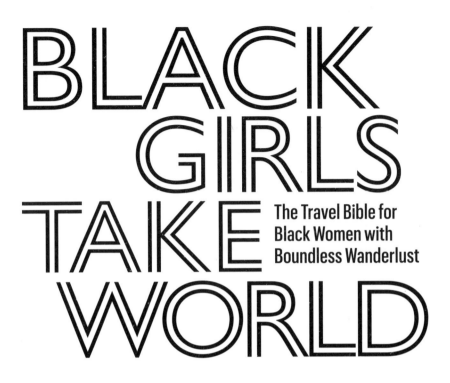

BLACK GIRLS GIRLS TAKE WORLD

The Travel Bible for
Black Women with
Boundless Wanderlust

Georgina Lawton

Illustrated by
Rachelle Baker

Hardie Grant

TRAVEL

BLACK GIRLS TAKE WORLD

Contents

INTRODUCTION

WHEN I WAS ASKED to write this travel guide, my initial thought was *Woo-hoo!* Tasked with creating a resource that included everything I've learned from my 14+ months of travelling alone, I had plans to write this book in Brazil or Bali with a cocktail in hand while I casually planned a route through heaving cities and verdant jungles, all in the name of research.

Then, the pandemic struck.

After years of preferring a life on the move, like many, I was forced to find solace in stillness. At first, it was difficult. But then I realised that such unprecedented times were ideal for writing and reflecting. This clarity of mind inspired conversations with some incredible wandering women, many of whom used the time in quarantine to do exciting things in the travel space and are featured within the pages of this book. And in taking time to think about how we have lost the traditional rituals of travel, I feel certain that

I hope we can continue to – safely – author our solo travel stories as black women, step boldly into the spaces of our daydreams and rise majestically into braver versions of ourselves.

many of us have gained a greater appreciation for our role as globetrotters.

As a black woman, I'm much more grateful for the privilege my British passport has afforded me since movement has been restricted. I talk more about this in the Travelling While Black chapter (*see* p. 123), but as black women, our relationship with passport privilege is complex. At home, we must contend with layers of discrimination and othering, but abroad, we are imbued with a smug pomposity, breezing through customs undisturbed and knowing we will be understood when we speak English.

Moving through the world in this way is a privilege many of our white counterparts are used to. Yet during the pandemic, the freedom that comes with owning a passport from a Western country has been eroded. As our lives were put on momentary pause and other countries imposed travel restrictions, the value of once-coveted passports like my own declined.

It's hard to imagine ever travelling with the same carefree abandon again. But I hope this period of relative stillness against the backdrop of Brexit, border rows and the battleground for racial justice will serve to remind each of us that travel is integral to widening our world. It teaches us about the country we are currently in and the country we are from, which shapes us into more conscientious, empathetic beings. As black women, we are certainly under no obligation to educate others about our lives, but when we are able to travel, we automatically dismantle the structural barriers that have held us back and understand that humanity's commonalities far outweigh the tiny differences that divide us. As Mark Twain once said, 'Travel is fatal to prejudice, bigotry and narrow-mindedness.'

In the months and years to come, I hope we can continue to – safely – author our solo travel stories as black women, step boldly into the spaces of our daydreams and rise majestically into braver versions of ourselves. I hope you are welcomed into corners of the globe that once seemed impossible to reach and that this book inspires you to embark on boundless and purposeful travel.

About the author

Georgina Lawton is a 20-something travel writer, author of the memoir, *Raceless*, and host of the Audible podcast, *The Secrets in Us*. As a journalist and columnist, her work has been published in *Guardian Weekend*, *The Independent*, *The i Paper*, *Stylist*, *gal-dem*, *Travel + Leisure*, *VICE*, *Time Out London* and more. Georgina has missed only two flights in her lifetime, her favourite continent is South America, her favourite cuisine is Thai and her remaining bucket list contains absolutely no bungee jumping.

Follow Georgina on
Twitter: @GeorginaLawton
Instagram: @georginalawton_

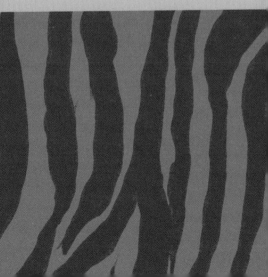

CHAPTER 1
Solo black female travel: The future

SOLO BLACK FEMALE TRAVEL: THE FUTURE

For black women, solo travel is a radical act, a tool of rebellion, an allegory for emancipation.

**OLO TRAVEL** is about creating opportunities on your own. It's about relying on yourself to seek out incredible adventures and make unforgettable memories that last far longer than the photos on your camera. Solo travel demands that you become your own source of joy and inspiration; it forces growth and independence. It requires you to constantly show up for, and be comfortable with, yourself.

When you travel unaccompanied or without much of a plan (in my opinion, there's no other way to do it), you quickly learn to shed layers of fear and uncertainty until the intense impetus to live life on your own terms becomes your ultimate driving force. Eventually you will find a bigger, bolder, more brilliant you at your very core. And if you do it right, this moment of inner reckoning should take place somewhere very idyllic.

Solo travel can be freeing and restorative, a chance to hit the restart button or a break to bring you back in touch with yourself. You may return home with not just a deeper understanding of a place and its people but of who you are – and I know from experience how valuable that is.

At 21 years old, I left London to roam the world alone for more than a year. I had recently lost my father and a large part of my identity, and travel was the medium I chose to repair myself with. I swayed to samba in the beating heart of Rio de Janeiro, ate mouth-watering street food in Vietnam and Mexico that sated my stomach and soul, wandered around ancient metropolises built on archaic customs in Morocco and lost days and a few nights (ahem!) in fleeting romantic encounters, divided by language but united by desire. I swam with seals in the Galapagos Islands, walked with white rhinos in Zimbabwe, was sunburned in Manhattan (yeah, not sure how that one happened), got debilitating food poisoning in Nicaragua, lost a DSLR camera in the Dominican Republic and nearly got arrested in Cuba.

Spending my time (and most of my money) on an extended period of solo travel is absolutely the best decision I have ever made. It helped me glue the pieces of myself back together, inspired my writing and reminded me of my place in a vibrant global diaspora. It was also a ridiculous amount of fun!

I've heard many black women offer protestations about why we should not travel solo, the terrible things that may happen to us, what we might lose by leaving our homes. And hey, I get the hesitation; there are times when I've felt on edge or unwelcome on the road. But for the most part, solo travel has given me far more than it has taken away, and it has always reminded me of my power in a world that so often serves to make me, as a black woman, feel small and powerless.

For far too long, black women have been told how to live. We have been forced to exist in spaces that were not built with our comfort in mind, and as such, we have absorbed the pernicious myths about our bodies, telling ourselves, 'No, I can't do that' or 'No, I don't belong here'. We have been denied the authorship to our travel stories and have been turned away or told to go home when we dared to demand more from our leisure time. But what would happen if you ignored the naysayers and the stereotypes? What would happen if, instead of waiting for permission or allowing fear to dictate your decisions, you simply told yourself, 'Yep, it's time for me to go'? What would happen if you took a leap of faith and booked that damn trip, B? I'm willing to bet you'd have the time of your life.

*Solo travel has given
me far more than it
has taken away.*

*Us solo females should
conquer the world
be accompanied
partner or*

—Oneika Raymond,

*go out there and
and not wait to
by a friend,
relative.*

ournalist and travel blogger

"

For black women, solo travel holds a deep meaning that's rooted in both the political and the personal. For centuries, the movement of black bodies has been strictly controlled. But why is black female leisure so radical? Well, during the brutal period of colonial expansion, black people were forcibly removed from African and Caribbean countries and transported across the globe for the economic advancement of white European nations. Black bodies were simply a tool for capitalist production, a means to an end, and as such, our access to leisure travel was denied. Rest days weren't exactly scheduled into the slavery timetable.

The movement of the black female body was (and still is) heavily policed. In times of bondage, we persevered, but we could not travel freely or for pleasure; such a concept would have directly contradicted colonial rule. And even though this period has long since ended, black women have inherited a legacy of narrow and biased assumptions about our bodies that impact us today. Neo-liberal capitalism and structural discrimination continue to burden black women more pertinently than many other groups. The systems we navigate are tainted by white supremacy and have never been designed for our self-discovery or pleasure. Opting out of this oppressive system via some well-deserved rest or leisure travel is actually pretty revolutionary. Therefore, black female travel can therefore be seen as a radical act, a tool of rebellion, an allegory for emancipation that allows us to redefine our position in the world.

To travel while black and female is to upend and overcome legacies of mobility impairment. It is to dispel myths that come from a history of restricted movement. It is to say, 'Boy, bye!' to a lifetime of setbacks and struggles. Now that might sound like a heavy load for lil' ole you to bear but I'm not implying that the route to racial equality rests on your

decision to visit Venice for the weekend. Just think of it as another thing to motivate you to book your trip.

Of course, in the age of the coronavirus, solo travel looks a little...different. You may be feeling more comfortable in your solitude, and the idea of travelling alone seems a little more appealing. Or perhaps you're so over working from home (I feel ya) and have realised that a digital nomad life is well within your reach now that your office has gone remote and freedom of location is no longer restricted to just freelancers. But if you've weighed up the risks and decided that travel is wholly necessary, now might actually be the best time to embark on that epic solo journey because things are cheaper and quieter *and* you're going to be socially distancing from others anyway, meaning you'll get a taste of true solitude.

We travel for ourselves, first and foremost, but attached to our journeys is the potential to rebuke stereotypes, break moulds, trace roots, foster inclusivity and give back.

Coronavirus is making us all rethink the purpose and pleasure behind solo travel. Psychologically, there's a shift in how we view people. Where the solo traveller once revelled in serendipitous moments with strangers, they must now limit their spontaneous interactions with them. Where we once saw others as potential friends, we must now think of them as potential virus carriers. Last-minute bookings have been replaced with meticulous research around location-specific safety precautions. Extreme planning is suddenly vital for safety – oh, and festivals, finger food and mask-free travel are now a distant myth from a time gone by!

In the world of travel, things have irrevocably changed. And while global tourism won't completely rebound for some time, there are travel deals aplenty to entice us to start exploring safely. Road-tripping at home is taking off, while popular tourist spots are once again unspoilt. On a trip to Lisbon in 2020, I snagged a bargain flight from the UK then found that the usual extra charges for one-person bookings on my walking tour had been scrapped.

Solo travel won't cease to exist in the era of COVID-19, but it will undoubtedly be shaped by the world's response to this health crisis for years to come. Still, I'm confident solo travellers can adapt (if there's one thing black women are it's damn resourceful).

Black women travelling the world freely and for pleasure is certainly boundary breaking – even more so if we manage to pull it off in a post-COVID world. And with the resurgence of the Black Lives Matter movement and a more urgent global discourse on the treatment of black bodies, now is an exciting (if not wildly unpredictable) time to add your experiences to a discourse steeped in revolutionary history.

THE BLACK TRAVEL movement began in 2013 as a social media-led conversation focused on greater visibility for adventurers who don't fit the traditional mould. It has since gone mainstream, with black-owned brands like Travel Noire, We Go Too, Tastemakers Africa and Nomadness Travel Tribe offering curated content, aspirational trips and heritage tourism to Africa, giving black consumers and travel providers a seat at the table while centring our stories.

So it seems like travelling solo for leisure is a privilege that more black women have been able to enjoy in recent years. We travel for escapism, excitement and unbridled joy, for the fun, the freedom and the food (the travel 10 is real). We travel for the nostalgia-inducing sunsets on secret beaches, the unmistakable feel of the wind in our fros and the hypnotic chant of a new city in our ears. We travel because we are lucky enough to venture to places our parents never could, to live out the dreams and intentions of our ancestors and be a part of a generation for whom free movement is finally feasible.

We travel to craft our personal identities, especially in spaces where being an unaccompanied woman of colour is seen as taboo. And we understand, better than most, the responsibility and consciousness related to our movement. We travel for ourselves, first and foremost, but attached to our journeys is the potential to rebuke stereotypes, break moulds, trace roots, foster inclusivity and give back. We travel *because we can*. And that in and of itself is enough of a reason to go.

Within the pages of this book, you'll mainly find writings by me, a world traveller and journalist who aims to convince you that solo travel is possible, no matter your personality type, bank balance or travel style. Also included are perspectives from some dope explorers whose knowledge extends far beyond my own: Jessica Nabongo, a Ugandan-American adventurer, who, in 2019, became the first black woman to visit every country in the world; Annette Richmond, an award-winning African American digital nomad and founder of Fat Girls Traveling; Sasha Sarago, editor of *Ascension* magazine for Aboriginal-Australian women, and Rhiane Fatinikun, founder of the British group Black Girls Hike. I hope our combined knowledge inspires your individual path to total travel freedom and encourages you to cast yourself in the lead role of your very own magical travel movie.

We travel because we are lucky enough to venture to places our parents never could, to live out the dreams and intentions of our ancestors.

Don't wait around
to be happy for you.
get you've got to

for other people
Any happiness you
make yourself.

—Alice Walker, author

CHAPTER 2
The travel hitlist

THE TRAVEL HITLIST

Good travel experiences can occur anywhere at any time.

WHETHER YOU'RE looking to lose yourself in a heaving urban metropolis in Europe, find yourself on a soul-boosting meditative trip in Asia or put those intrepid explorer skills to the test with a wildlife adventure in South America, these recommendations will tease out your inner explorer and inspire your true travel purpose.

These lists are general; I've stayed away from grouping entire countries in round-ups as 'safe' or 'unsafe' for black women, such as 'The top 10 countries for black women to travel to'. I believe such lists are reductive, suggesting that entire nations spanning thousands of square miles and containing millions of different people should be avoided by black women to ensure their safety, and that inversely, there are countries to which we should flock en masse because they will guarantee us a great experience. That just simply ain't true! Good travel experiences can occur anywhere at any time, and there is no such thing as a dangerous country, only dangerous individuals.

This is a sentiment shared by Jessica Nabongo, otherwise known as The Catch Me If You Can across social media. Jessica is something of a travel legend. Why? Well, because in 2019, she became the first black woman to travel to every country in the world, and she also runs a successful boutique travel agency called Jet Black, which focuses on travel beyond Europe. Her travel knowledge runs deep, but she's also aware of how boring and binary discussions about solo travel can be.

*There is no
such thing as a
dangerous country,
only dangerous
individuals.*

'I don't believe in broad overviews of places,' she says. 'Round-ups on the best or worst countries for black people to travel to just instils fear. Every country in the world deserves nuance.'

She adds, 'I've been to 195 countries, but the scary things that have happened to me are far and few between. I still get people asking me what places are safest for black people, but it is individual people who are racist or sexist. Of course, anti-blackness exists on a global level, but why not take negative stories we hear with a grain of salt in the same way we take positive stories?'

Once again for the people in the back!

The tips in this travel hitlist are based on personal experiences from my time travelling the world alone (unless I've specified that it comes from another travel expert). So all that's left for you is to decide what kind of trip you're feelin'. Happy planning!

HITLIST TOP 5
European city breaks

A wealth of cultural history, gloriously diverse natural landscapes and some seriously weird and wacky nightlife means Europe's cities hold something for everyone. Dive in and explore.

5 Berlin, Germany

The beating heart of Berlin, Germany, is a firm favourite among party-loving travellers in search of creative and cultural adventures. Despite what you may have heard, black people are the country's most visible minority, and Berlin is

Culture does no[
People make[

—Chimamanda Ngoz[

...make people.
...culture.

Adichie, author

as diverse as it is lively, attracting hipsters and history buffs alike. Floor-shaking house and techno music is ubiquitous in big clubs like Wilde Renate, Watergate, Sisyphos and the ever-exclusive Berghain, but of course, Berlin offers more than just beats and bars.

Head north to the bathing lakes of Brandenburg for the perfect antidote to urban life, visit the Berlin Wall and all its street art at the East Side Gallery, or head to The Stasi Museum (my favourite educational spot that charts the rise and role of Berlin's secret police) and the Jewish Museum for further fascinating glimpses into the city's storied past.

> **HITLIST TIP:** *Ebe Ano serves incredible Nigerian soul food, and Natural Hair Berlin is great if you run out of afro hair products.*

> **HITLIST TIP:** *Stay in the artsy area of Kreuzberg for easy access to the rest of the city and cool vibes.*

4 Galway, Ireland

Voted the European Capital of Culture in 2020, Galway is both a cosmopolitan city getaway and a glorious gateway to breathtaking countryside along the Wild Atlantic Way. Boasting colourful pubs with 'trad sessions', i.e. live Irish music (Tig Cōili, Taaffes and The Front Door Pub being three popular spots), a thriving university community and a calendar of events as part of the Galway International Arts Festival each July, there's plenty of *craic* to be had for the wandering woman (and no, I'm not biased because I'm half-Irish!).

> **HITLIST TIP:** *Galway's bustling street market has global street food cuisine, plants and arts and crafts. Pre-COVID, the market was open all year round on Saturdays from 8am to 6pm and Sundays, bank holidays, Fridays in July and August and every day during the Galway Arts Festival from 12pm to 6pm.*

> **HITLIST TIP:** *Head 90 minutes south to County Clare for unspoilt Irish vistas. Experience the history of fossils, walk the otherworldly limestone pavements at the Burren, spot bottlenose dolphins in the deep blue mouth of the River Shannon and drink in dramatic views on the Cliffs of Moher.*

3 Florence, Italy

Florence, the capital of Italy's Tuscany region, is the definition of true romance, Renaissance and delectable cuisine. Visits to the terracotta-tiled Duomo di Milano Cathedral and the Uffizi art gallery (where you'll find masterpieces by Michelangelo, Da Vinci and Botticelli) are pretty much obligatory. And there's people-watching aplenty while strolling along the Arno River or with an aperitivo in one of the city's spectacular squares. Anecdotal travel experiences from black women vary greatly in Italy, but in Florence, you won't stand out and the locals are spirited. Be sure to check out the sprawling verdant hills of the Chianti wine region with one of the many day tours, or if you're on a budget, take a public bus to the sleepy town of Fiesole.

> **HITLIST TIP:** *Check the morning markets and locally run restaurants in Piazza Santo Spirito square. Bellísimo!*

2 Budapest, Hungary

You'd be hard-pressed to find a more chill and laidback city than the Hungarian capital of Budapest, which seamlessly blends the old and new on every corner and, as a result, constantly surprises. Take a scenic boat ride down the Danube River to marvel at the ancient architecture and Chain Bridge. Unwind like a local at a luxury bathhouse. Party at a famous 'ruin bar', where electronic music bounces from the crumbling walls of disused warehouses (the best are Szimpla Kert and Fogasház). Head to the impressive neo-Gothic Great Market Hall to grab a lángos, a traditional, deep-fried, disc-shaped bread covered in cream cheese and garlic (yes, please!). Budapest isn't renowned for its cultural diversity, but locals are polite and the city activities won't disappoint.

> **HITLIST TIP:** *By day, Szechenyi Baths offers spa treatments in the grandeur of a sprawling 20th-century Turkish spring, but on weekend nights, it hosts the 'sparty' - a raucous rave in a pool, not for the faint-hearted!*

> **HITLIST TIP:** *Most of the culinary and clubbing action takes place in the Jewish District. Don't miss Mazel Tov, a leafy, dreamy, open-air bar and restaurant that's serving up relaxed vibes and amazing Israeli-Mediterranean food.*

1 Lisbon, Portugal

Understated yet glamorous, Lisbon will seduce even the most hard-to-please solo strollers. Whether you want to savour a pastel de nata in a tiny blue-tiled cafe, traverse colourful cobblestone streets by bike or marvel at the ethereal architecture of a palace or three (Casa do Alentejo and Palácio Foz are impressive, while the nearby town of Sintra boasts several more), Lisbon has it all.

With music, food and culture from the city's Cape Verde, Mozambique and Angola inhabitants, the infectious energy may feel familiar. Don't miss Cantinho do Aziz, which serves Portuguese-Mozambique dishes, and the African Lisbon walking tour, which traces the city's colonial past.

> **HITLIST TIP:** *Lisbon is the City of Seven Hills, meaning there are spectacular views at almost every turn. Enjoy them from a rooftop bar like Lost in Esplanada, a vibrant spot with day beds and delicious local cuisine, or Park, where DJs and panoramic vistas go hand in hand.*

> **HITLIST TIP:** *Don't skip the coastline. The Costa da Caparica boasts 26km (16mi) of sparkling sandy beaches, and it's just a 30-minute drive from Lisbon.*

Understated yet glamorous, Lisbon seduces even the most hard to place solo strollers.

HITLIST TOP 3
Best North America and Caribbean trips

Find heaving metropolises alongside paradisiacal beaches in North America, the third largest continent in the world.

3 New York City, USA

OK, before I hear the collective groan from all my East Coast dwellers, allow me to explain. Maybe it's because I'm a Londoner, but I feel constantly enthralled by New York – our cooler, more stylish, more unbothered older cousin. Perhaps it's because a British accent goes really far there, or because it's a city of real extremes. Whatever the reason, NYC is an explorer's dream.

Beyond the obvious (Ellis Island boat tours, Williamsburg bar-hopping and Manhattan skyscrapers), you've got beauty in unexpected places, like the ceiling at Grand Central Terminal, golden hour on the Brooklyn Bridge, the iconic brownstones of Bedford-Stuyvesant, the subway buskers at lunch, the cocktail of various accents, the smell of corn dogs at Coney Island and the reassuring, 24/7 glare of the bodega lights on every corner. There are a million things to see and do in New York but also a million ways to make it yours.

2 Las Terrenas, Dominican Republic

Drenched in sunshine all year round, this former fishing village on the peninsula of Samaná is not as sleepy as it once was, but it's still a hell of a lot quieter than Punta Cana, the most popular spot on the island. I'll be honest, if you don't like near-unspoilt sands, turquoise seas and beach bar shacks serving coconut fish ceviche and fresh juice for a few dollars, you won't like Las Terrenas. The rhythm of daily life is slow, the people are so relaxed that they're horizontal and you can quite easily spend day after day on the sands or drinking yourself silly in the lively bars filled with a good mix of expats and locals. Sounds awful? Best leave it to me then...

1 Chiapas, Mexico

This southern mountainous state in Mexico is as surprising as it is diverse. There are ancient ruins and quaint towns drenched in indigenous culture. Bathed in jungle mist and surrounded by greenery are the Mayan ruins of Palenque, which is home to a temple that was occupied in the seventh century A.D. that can be explored in just a couple of hours. Head to San Cristóbal de las Casas for colonial architecture and kitsch markets (bring a jacket, even if it's summer). For natural vibes, take a tour into the heart of the Montes Azules Biosphere Reserve, a sprawling section of North America's remaining rainforest.

HITLIST TIP: *See my list of best hostels later in the book for amazing accommodations in San Cristóbal de las Casas.*

"

Never be limited by limited imaginations other people's wisdom, re-evaluate the world other people's ... You can hear but you've got to for yourself.

—Mae Jemison, astronaut

HITLIST TOP 5
Wildlife and adventure trips

Live out your jungle girl fantasies with these DIY and group trips from around the world.

5 Trek volcanoes in Ometepe, Nicaragua.

Ever considered Nicaragua? Often regarded as one of the safest tourist spots in Latin America, the countryside embraces intrepid explorers, and Ometepe is arguably the top spot for adventure. An ethereal island of two volcanoes that rise majestically out of Lake Nicaragua (the largest, Concepción, takes up to 10 hours to tackle, while Maderas takes eight), Ometepe is home to verdant scenery, lush lagoons and crystalline waterholes. Cool off in Ojo de Agua, a natural volcanic pool where you can spot birds, butterflies, squirrels and iguanas with a cocktail or coconut water in hand.

> **HITLIST TIP:** *Rent a scooter to whiz around the best parts of the island for around £20/$24 a day (not including petrol). Be mindful of the rocky roads!*

> **HITLIST TIP:** *There's a great choice of budget hostels and eco-lodges on Ometepe, but for a touch of opulence with an infinity pool overlooking a view of the volcanos, head to La Omaja Hotel.*

4 Explore the Caribbean coast of Colombia.

Colombia's sparkling jewel is its Caribbean coast. With African influences everywhere and a huge roster of adventures, it shouldn't be missed. Wander around colourful Cartagena, with its colonial architecture, raucous rooftop parties and fruit hawkers balancing bright fruits atop vibrant headpieces. Then, head to Barranquilla to drink aguardiente liquor in the streets while dancing salsa with locals during the annual February carnival.

Don't skip Santa Marta, a town largely known for its parties, empanada shops and incredible daytrip options, Minca being the most spectacular. The tiny hilltop town offers eco-lodges aplenty, such as Casa Elemento where you can spend an evening in a hammock and watch the sun fade behind cloud-covered mountains.

After years of political turmoil, Colombia is shrugging off its reputation as a nation unsuitable for tourists, and although there's petty crime, the Caribbean coast is bursting with so much *vida*, it's impossible not to love it.

HITLIST TIP: *If it's relaxation you're after, take a bus to Palomino, a sleepy former fishing town with yellow sands and a slow pace of life just one hour and 45 minutes from Santa Marta. Or if you fancy a hike, Ciudad Perdida (the Lost City) is an archaeological site from 650 years ago that can be tackled in three to four days.*

HITLIST TIP: *Tayrona National Park boasts monkeys, lizards, parrots and polar-white sands. You can camp overnight or soak up the scenery for a day.*

3 Safari across the savannah of Zimbabwe and South Africa.

An African safari provides up close exposure to awe-inspiring savannah wildlife while allowing you to mingle with other travellers. There's no better region than the unspoilt plains of South Africa and Zimbabwe to take part in these adventures. Go on a Geckos Adventure nine-day safari trip, and you'll benefit from included meals, accommodations and the expertise of local trip leaders.

You'll begin at Zimbabwe's stunning Victoria Falls (one of the Seven Natural Wonders of the World), where you'll have the chance to marvel at the majestic crashing curtain of water and misty rainbows. If you're an adrenaline junkie, you can fly 120m (395ft) across or into the gorge below with a choice of two incredible zip-lines or one bungee jump.

Head to the famous Hwange and Kruger National Parks and wake up to roaring lions outside your tent or experience the sights and sounds of one or all of the Big Five (lions, leopards, rhinos, elephants and buffalo). In Matobo National Park, there's also the chance to literally walk alongside endangered black rhinos at a local conservation camp. This is a totally unforgettable trip for animal-curious thrill-seekers.

HITLIST TIP: *Both zip-lines at Victoria Falls are definitely worth the nerves. The 110m (364ft) bungee jump, however? Well, that one requires a bit more courage...*

HITLIST TIP: *If you're planning on camping overnight at a safari park, keep in mind that they can be super remote. A torchlight (flashlight), books, spare toilet paper, snacks, warm clothes and mosquito repellent are all must-haves.*

2 Sail through the Amazon jungle in Brazil.

The Amazon rainforest spans 54.4 million km^2 (2.1 million mi^2) and more than nine countries, so knowing where to enter is key. Head to Manaus, the capital city of the Amazonas region in Brazil, for options like budget-friendly day-jungle tours, which increase in price for guide-accompanied options.

For something more immersive, Adventure Life's seven-night 'Voyage to the Heart of the Amazon' trip brings you into untouched and uninhabited rainforest via a comfortable motor yacht equipped with a hammock-lined deck and 70 glass windows. Kayak across the tar-black waters of the River Negro before breakfast while listening for howler monkeys in the canopy above. Glide through the swamp-like world of the flooded forest in a canoe as you watch sea-blue

In the Amazon jungle you can kayak across the tar-black waters of the River Negro while listening for howler monkeys in the canopy above.

butterflies and toucans flutter past. Enjoy serene walks among thick trees and deserted beaches, where you can spot pink dolphins (yep, they exist) and fish for piranha on still waters. Prepare for your spine to tingle during the night-time caiman and sloth expeditions. Besides the boat crew, you won't see another soul for days, and once you get back to civilization, you may just miss waking up to the sounds of the jungle.

> **HITLIST TIP:** *The Amazon is so dense, it can be extremely tricky to spot the wildlife! A good guide and a reputable tour company are a must for making the most of your experience - oh, and some damn good binoculars!*

1 Swim with stingrays and sharks in the Galápagos Islands, Ecuador.

For breathtaking biodiversity, nowhere beats the Galápagos Islands, a volcanic archipelago of 21 islands in the Pacific Ocean, 1000km (600mi) off the coast of Ecuador. This group of islands inspired Charles Darwin's research in 1835 and provides up close and personal sights of rare wildlife. Flights from the mainland take about three hours, and cruises are always readily available. You can also organise daytrips to three of the most popular islands: Santa Cruz, a lush, relaxing getaway with incredible snorkelling at Camaño Island and loads of sea lions; Isabela, which is home to thousands of colourful iguanas, swooping pelicans, blue-footed booby birds, super-cute penguins and 500lb tortoises at The Giant Tortoise Breeding Centre; and San Cristóbal, which is home to nesting frigates and León Dormido Bay, the perfect area to swim alongside sea turtles, manta rays and sharks.

Here, island guides are mandatory, so choose a reputable tour like Intrepid's 'Best of Galápagos', which is 10 days long and includes a wealth of natural world knowledge, expertly led boat trips and a volcano trek, as well as other accommodations.

> **HITLIST TIP**: *Pack well and pack responsibly! Your bags get searched every time you swap islands to prevent the disturbance of fragile ecosystems. Don't try and sneak any shells off the beach.*

> **HITLIST TIP**: *Pay attention! The Galápagos Islands are home to some of the highest levels of endemism anywhere on the earth, meaning 80% of the land birds and 97% of the reptiles and land mammals can only be found there. Every sight is a once-in-a-lifetime opportunity.*

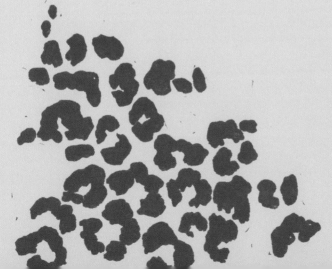

HITLIST TOP 6
Rest and rejuvenation trips

Need a solo trip to restore your zen? I got you, girl!

6 Lake Bled, Slovenia

In northwest Slovenia sits a turquoise lake surrounded by stunning mountains and forests, the perfect setting to recharge your batteries. Lake Bled boasts the picturesque Bled Castle, which sits atop the rocky peaks of the Julian Alps. While it's super relaxing during the off season, in the summer months, this place is packed.

Rent a bike and cycle around the area to take in the scenic views, nab a slice of Bled's famous cream cake at a cafe and if it's warm, find a sandy bank and take a dip in the perfect blue waters.

HITLIST TIP: *Head to Lake Bohinj for a swim if you can't find a secluded spot near the main lake during the busy season.*

5 Chiang Mai, Thailand

Situated in Northern Thailand, peaceful Chiang Mai offers a relaxing antidote to the country's bustling capital of Bangkok. This walkable city offers a soporific pace of life, where the old mixes with the new in the form of ancient buildings beside bustling co-working spaces and vibrant food markets. Be sure to visit Nimmanhaemin Road for art galleries and cute cafes, and venture over to the 14th-century Wat Phra Singh Buddhist temple to take in the impressive architecture.

Get up close and personal with nature at the ethically run elephant nature park, pamper yourself at one of the city's many spa parlours or marvel at the very strong reggae/Rastafarian vibe that threads through many of the bars (yes, really).

4 Porto, Portugal

Porto is often overshadowed by its more glamorous older sister Lisbon, but it lends itself to a more peaceful vibe with its quiet, candle-lit bars, serene cruises down the Douro and enchanting neighbourhoods.

Meander through the narrow, cobbled streets of Rua da Reboleira, where you can people-watch with a port in hand, or head five minutes further south to enjoy live music and a fresh, fish-filled dinner by the water. Pick up a book at Livraria Lello, the dramatic, neo-Gothic library that inspired J.K Rowling's Hogwarts, and hop on the quick but impressive Elevador da Ribeira for panoramic views of the city.

3 Mirissa, Sri Lanka

This sleepy town in Southern Sri Lanka offers an appealing pace of life with chic bars, clean sands and far less people than Unawatuna, a nearby popular beach town. Surfing, snorkelling and whale-watching are all easy activities to get into at Mirissa Beach, but if you want something slightly quieter, head to Secret Beach, just a five-minute tuk-tuk ride from the centre of town (it's actually not so much of a secret during the busy season, but it's swim-friendly and somewhat serene).

Coconut Tree Hill is a great spot to take stunning tree-lined photos (again, get there super early to avoid crowds), and if you're still not sufficiently relaxed, book a traditional Ayurvedic massage at a local spa.

> **HITLIST TIP**: *Take a daytrip to Galle, a UNESCO World Heritage site. This colonial fort town with Dutch and Portuguese influences is an eclectic mix of fine dining restaurants, gift shops, jewellers and art galleries.*

2 Rotorua, New Zealand

Relax in all-natural Rotorua. With its sulphuric air, bubbling mud pools and natural hot springs, it's something of a geothermal wonderland. This travel destination tip comes from Sasha Sarago, founder of Ascension, Australia's first digital lifestyle platform for women of colour. Sasha raises awareness around colourism, identity and Aboriginal Australian rights, and says she was blown away by Rotorua's mellow, natural vibe and the way the indigenous population, the Māori people, is treated there.

'The Māori culture is everywhere in Rotorua, and there is a deep respect and love for it,' she notes. 'And the spas are very natural and use natural minerals from the earth. The respect for nature and the land is embedded in everything there.'

She notes that in addition to hiking and mud baths, there are adventure sports aplenty, like parasailing, zip-lining and white water rafting.

We need to reshape
perception of how
ourselves. We have
as women and take

—Beyoncé Knowles, singer

our own

ve view

o step up

the lead.

and songwriter

"

1 Ubud, Bali, Indonesia

Known as the 'Island of the Gods', Bali is not just a city; it's more of a state of eternal chill. The enduring appeal of the northern town Ubud is largely attributed to the traditional Balinese culture that oozes from every corner, the hypnotic chants wafting from ornate Hindu temples, the ridiculously friendly locals and the calming sight of unending verdant jungle.

Ubud is fairly touristic, packed with more yoga retreats and work spaces than you can shake a stick at, but if you pick accommodations outside of the bustling town centre, you'll succumb to the area's spiritual charm. Who could say no to a ritual purification bath in the waters of the Tirta Empul Temple or the breathtaking views from the Tegallalang rice fields? Rest and rejuvenation is inevitable.

Clean, delicious eating and culinary innovation can be found in Ubud's many cafes and restaurants, which are a whole mood in and of themselves. Milk & Madu offers ambrosial banana bread in the hippest of settings, Clear Café is adorned with flowers and filled with soothing indoor ponds and IBU SUSU serves unbeatable crispy crab.

There are many things to do in Ubud, but if you do none of them and simply spend your time strolling around temples and eating well, you'll have had a successful trip in my opinion.

> **HITLIST TIP:** *The best massage of your life (and an Insta-worthy flower bath) awaits you at Karsa Spa.*

> **HITLIST TIP:** *Rent a moped to explore the entire island in a new way.*

HITLIST TOP 4
Cities for fun and fiestas

It's impossible to be bored in these perpetually happening places. To borrow Drake's words, it's a case of 'more life, more everything'. Enjoy!

4 Fez, Morocco

Visiting the city of Fez is a lot like being inside a really vivid dream. The history of this city dates back to the eighth century and is a dazzling patchwork of African, European and Arab culture. Be sure to wander through the UNESCO-protected, maze-like medina (the ancient walled part of the city), a warren of old alleys, vibrant souks (markets) and gorgeous riads (houses).

Best explored with a local guide, it's here you'll spot donkeys and carts squeezing through crumbling alleys, locals weaving through tunnels with bread on their heads and markets selling live chickens and hand-woven tapestries. Warning: the medina is a lot, but the city's spectacular palaces, spas and gardens will work like a tonic on your soul after a long day of walking around. Be sure to visit Jardin Jnan Sbil, a tranquil oasis of palm trees, eucalyptus, weeping willows, bamboo and water, located in the centre of Fez.

> **HITLIST TIP:** *Eat at the popular Darori Resto in the medina. An exquisitely prepared menu for two in this gorgeous riad costs around £23/$27 (300 dirhams). For a fun mix of live music, culture and Moroccan-Euro food, try the ever-popular Café Clock.*

3 Havana, Cuba

Are you ready to be seduced by time-warped Cuba? It may happen quickly in Havana, where the Spanish is fast and casual, the women call you *mi vida* (my life) and the salsa pours from every window.

Stay in La Habana Vieja, the enchanting old quarter, and you'll see 1950s Chevrolets beside towering carts of fruits and vegetables with live music playing on every corner. Stay at Hostel Mango to meet other travellers or, for a real taste of Cuba, sleep in a traditional homestay, known as a *casa particular*, available to book on Homestay.com or through word of mouth and email. Mingle with locals by the Malecon wall, the epicentre of the city where drinking, singing and chatting take on a romantic feel by the water. Grab a mojito at Ernest Hemmingway's former watering hole, El Floridita, or dance at Fábrica de Arte Cubano, a huge, hip art gallery/club outside the city that offers live music and cultural events.

Don't sleep on Havana's beaches either. Ice-white sands are just 30 minutes away at Santa María del Mar beach. Grab the A40 bus to travel like a local or pick up a *colectivo* (group taxi). Leave several days to take in the magic and mayhem of this majestic city.

HITLIST TIP: *If you want to blend in and save money, pick up the local currency, known as 'moneda nacional', or CUP, from a bureau de change. It can be used for street food and tipping; a pizza from a local cafe will set you back just 15 CUP, around 40p/70c.*

2 Accra, Ghana

This destination tip comes from travel entrepreneur Jessica Nabongo, who has travelled to 195 countries on her own and favours the African continent above all others. Jessica recommends Accra for its 'amazing art, gorgeous cuisine and lots of really, really high-end bars and restaurants'. One of which is Sky Bar, a rooftop venue that offers panoramic views of the city on a book-only basis.

Although Jessica notes that traffic in Accra is 'crazy', tourism within the country has boomed in recent years after the government announced 2019 as 'the year of return' for anyone within the diaspora looking to reconnect with their roots. So it looks like this is as good a time as any to check out everything Ghana has to offer.

For a real taste of Cuba, sleep in a traditional homestay, known as a casa particular.

1 Rio de Janeiro, Brazil

Despite the deep class and racial struggles that thread through the fabric of Brazil, Rio de Janeiro's dynamic and adaptive community is the beating heart of the city. Visit for Carnival, and you'll experience the soul-enriching pleasure of writhing and dancing in a samba-fuelled sea of black and brown bodies and learn exactly why Cariocas (the people of Rio) have earnt the reputation of having an insatiable lust for life.

When you've ticked off the other must-dos within the Marvellous City (hiking Sugarloaf Mountain, checking out the Christ the Redeemer statue, walking the mosaic steps of Escadaria Selarón or people-watching on Copacabana Beach, for example), remember to support the many black street artists and performers you'll see around. Buy their art, tip them properly and book accommodations through Diaspora. Black, a sort of black Airbnb. Or you can stay at black-owned Casa Cool Beans in the artsy neighbourhood of Santa Teresa.

HITLIST TOP 8
Best hostels and homestays around the world

Contrary to folklore (and some early noughties blogs), hostels can actually be cool. Most are clean, safe and social, offering private or shared accommodation alongside communal living or gaming areas.

I've turned to hostels on my travels to keep costs down and connect with like-minded travellers. Even if you think you won't like it, trust me when I say there's a hostel for everyone. Whether you're after a party atmosphere or something more low-key, whether you want a women's-only accommodation or an LGBTQIA+-friendly hostel, with a little research and prior planning, you can find one that suits your travel needs. Booking direct is sometimes cheaper than using Hostelworld or HostelBookers, and it's always important to search the reviews for keywords that match your requirements (i.e., 'air-con' or 'breakfast') so you know what to expect.

I've shared my space with many strangers over the years, and these days, if I'm alone on the road and feeling sociable, I still turn to hostels to ensure I connect with people like me. However, I'm now more inclined to book myself into a private room; that way, I get my own space but can still benefit from the atmosphere in the communal areas. Oh, and here are a few things that are essential to make your hostel stay more comfortable:

- Ear plugs
- Eye mask
- Universal adapter
- Flip-flops
- Hanging wash bag
- Sleeping bag liner

Looking for a little hostel inspiration? Here are my recommendations for the best in the world.

8 L'Auberge Inn Hostel in Quito, Ecuador
Clean, quiet and safe with comfortable rooms, this centrally located Quito hostel is a great place to explore more of the city.

7 Hostel Mango in Havana, Cuba
Run by a down-to-earth Cuban couple that's full of handy tips and tricks for getting around the country, Hostel Mango is one of the only dorm spaces in Havana, and it works out cheaper than a traditional homestay. Breakfast is included and private rooms are available.

These days, if I'm alone on the road and feeling sociable, I still turn to hostels to ensure I connect with people like me.

6 Casa Elemento in Santa Marta, Colombia

Does waking up in a treehouse to the sunrise melting into the never-ending greenery of the Sierra Nevada de Santa Marta mountains sound like a good morning to you? If so, a stay at this popular hostel is mandatory. Book well in advance.

5 Blue Trailz in Tamarindo, Costa Rica

Whether you want surfing lessons or an opportunity to go on incredible excursions, this laidback, Dutch-run hostel is a tropical oasis that's moments from the beach and situated within the party town of Tamarindo.

4 Hanoi City Backpackers Hostel in Hanoi, Vietnam

One of the more lively hostels, Hanoi City Backpackers has a buzzing bar and arranges incredible excursions all around Vietnam with rooms that are safe and secure – all for a reasonable price.

3 The Dreamer Hostel in Palomino, Colombia

A hostel that feels more like a luxury resort, The Dreamer is located on Palomino's sands and offers an outdoor pool surrounded by lush greenery, the perfect base to explore more of Colombia's incredible Caribbean coast.

2 Island Life Hostel in Santo Domingo, Dominican Republic

This award-winning, British-Dominican-run hostel is situated in the historic Zona Colonial and offers a shared gaming area, hot tub, hammock-lined garden and pool, as well as rooms equipped with lockers and storage. A total must-visit if you're on the island.

1 Posada del Abuelito in San Cristóbal de las Casas, Mexico

More than just a hostel, Posada del Abuelito is a whole Latin lifestyle – cosy, rustic, authentic. The colourful, flower-filled courtyard feels like a scene from a movie, the hearty breakfast of artisanal bread and homemade jam is a fabulous touch and the rooms are chic and comfy and come with extra blankets if needed. No wonder this hostel has been voted one of the best in the world time and time again.

"

*It [is] about
amongst ourselves
one another*

—Evita Robinson, founder

creating space for us to celebrate and travel.

of Nomadness Travel Tribe

Q&A WITH
Jessica Nabongo

Instagram: @thecatchmeifyoucan
Website: thecatchmeifyoucan.com

In 2019, Ugandan-American, Detroit-based travel entrepreneur Jessica Nabongo became the first black woman to travel to 195 countries. She owns her own boutique travel company, Jet Black, which focuses on providing individuals and brands with deep cultural dives and luxury travel.

What advice can you give to apprehensive wannabe solo travellers?
You need to ask: what are you afraid of? Whether I'm a woman or black, there's no need to be afraid because I believe everyone is my neighbour. I don't say, 'This country is unsafe for women or black people' because it instills fear in people. There's good and bad everywhere.

It's important to decolonise travel, and that means getting people to go to other countries and value them in the same way they do Europe and Asia.

What's your favourite continent?
Give me Africa all day long! Asia is my second favourite, as it's super diverse and the food is amazing.

What's been your favourite wildlife trip?
Whale-watching north of Norway in December was incredible. It's dusk all the time in winter, and you're on a speedboat in Arctic temperatures. It's a really unique experience.

What country did you unexpectedly love?
I really enjoyed Uzbekistan. Russia was also great. I'm unmistakably black, and there's a lot of discussion around racism in these places, but for me, they were amazing.

How do you choose your perfect travel destination?

I like to go places where I'm the only foreigner, as it feels more authentic. There's so much beauty in the unknown. In Thailand, I loved Chiang Mai way more than Phuket or Bangkok. I also like to go somewhere I haven't seen all over Instagram. Petra in Jordan was way more interesting than Machu Picchu just because I hadn't seen it everywhere.

How has COVID-19 changed the way we travel?

I think we will see an increase in travel to Africa because of their low amount of COVID cases, but it will be interesting to see if governments put the revenue from tourism over the safety of the people.

Do you believe the travel industry needs to be less Eurocentric?

Definitely. It's important to decolonise travel, and that means getting people to go to other countries and value them in the same way they do Europe and Asia, not just through 'voluntourism' and missions. Why don't we value African cities and cuisine in the same way we value European ones? Beyond safari tours, there is amazing art, restaurants and delicious cuisine in Africa. It's rare you see a black or a brown country being mentioned in any list of the top cuisines in the world.

What are your favourite African cities?

Dakar in Senegal – the food is so good and fresh. Nairobi's art scene is dope, and there's really good creative scenes. Addis Ababa - I love Ethiopian food. Lagos is phenomenal, but for people who have never been to Africa, it's a difficult city to deal with!

CHAPTER 3

How *not* to be basic when travelling

HOW NOT TO BE BASIC WHEN TRAVELLING

You can satiate your travel bug and travel responsibly at the same time, ya know!

**VER HEARD THAT** one about leaving a place in a better state than you found it? Well, if you implement a few of these tips as a solo traveller, you may be able to do just that.

These dos and don'ts are designed to get you thinking deeper about your place in the world and your impact on others, as well as how you can stay safe. I hope they might inspire you to simply travel better, whether that looks like improving your haggling skills, thinking more seriously about eco-travel or just avoiding reckless situations when dating abroad. You can satiate your travel bug while travelling responsibly, ya know! But recently, that's taken on a new meaning. Travel during the pandemic requires careful consideration and forward planning, and nowadays, travel starts as soon as you leave the house; but somewhat luckily I guess, the same precautions you take for going to the grocery store are the same ones needed for train or plane travel – masks, social distancing, handwashing and minimised contact. These are all things that are part of our new normal to keep ourselves and others safe, and they can be implemented into our travel, no matter how long the trip.

Of course, before travelling anywhere now you must first assess your risk of exposure to COVID-19, calculating whether your trip poses a risk to others and if you would have access to health care in a worst-case scenario. Pandemic travel requires extra work and planning, but it should serve as even more of an impetus to leave your basic bitch tendencies at *home*. Stay diligent and self-aware, and you should stay safe.

In the aftermath of a global health crisis that has hit small businesses, buying local is helpful.

Do think about how you interact with indigenous groups.

Taking part in a tour of an indigenous community can be done respectfully with a little research and forward planning. Sasha Sarago, of Wadjanbarra Yidinji, Jirrbal (Australian Aboriginal) and African American heritage, explains that a voyeuristic tour isn't always the best way to engage with these communities.

'I think it's more purposeful to give money rather than ask marginalised groups to produce something for me as a tourist. I don't want them to give me a show or gifts. I want them to share stories on their terms, not because they have to.'

Do support local businesses.

In the aftermath of a global health crisis that will undoubtedly hit small-scale enterprises within the tourism industry the hardest, buying local is wise. That may mean arranging a staycation instead of a trip overseas, buying fruits and veggies from local markets over chain supermarkets, frequenting guesthouses and homestays over conglomerate hotels, eating at small cafes and restaurants instead of chains, supporting self-employed tour guides, taxi drivers, artists and musicians, not being a tight-ass with tips, leaving online reviews for stand-out experiences and choosing tour companies that support small organisations.

Do haggle respectfully.

I get it; the allure of a holiday market can be irresistible. Everyone wants to snap up a handmade beaded purse for a rock-bottom price, but don't lose yourself and over-haggle, as Annette Richmond, founder of Fat Girls Traveling, notes.

It [is] about breaking
but also socioeconomic
people know that they
rich, white, and affluen.

—Evita Robinson, founder o

not only racial bounds, letting didn't need to be to see the world.

Nomadness Travel Tribe

'American money can be a lot abroad, so don't try and get a ridiculously low price just because you can; that's disrespectful,' she advises.

If you aren't sure on quality or if you just fancy a bargain, knowing how to haggle is important. Before you begin, shop around so you know what a reasonable price is for that product. Always be sure on the currency. If you don't know the exchange rate or understand the difference between 100 Cuban CUC and CUP, you will get ripped off – and don't expect to get a refund, boo!

Compliment the products, engage in a little cultural exchange, and you'll find it so much easier to haggle – and quite literally – secure the bag.

Don't be a travel snob.

Travelling for pleasure is a privilege. Remember that not everyone has the same travel tastes, and many others will not aspire to travel solo like you. One person's ideal travel style may be another person's private hell, so don't scoff, don't show off and don't country count; it's lame!

Do plan ahead in the era of a pandemic.

In the era of the COVID-19 pandemic, planning really is prevention. Healthcare practices vary from country to country, so always research how your chosen destination is handling things. Are masks required in shops? Are restaurants serving indoors? Is your insurance policy valid there? Don't endanger yourself and others by not planning ahead.

If you're flying, remember that snacks and drinks aren't readily available at airports and on the plane to minimise contact. Pack your own, as well as a reusable water bottle and a pen to fill out airline landing cards (giving out pens to passengers wasn't allowed on my Lisbon flight in 2020).

Travelling for pleasure is a privilege. Remember that not everyone has the same travel tastes, and many others will not aspire to travel solo like you.

> *Forgo the geisha costumes in Japan, forget the fake moustaches for Cinco de Mayo and don't imitate Native Americans by wearing headdresses.*

Do wear the right kit.

As Rhiane Fatinikun of Black Girls Hike notes, being prepared with the right kit is vitally important for keeping safe, warm and dry. 'There's a lot of choice but don't get put off by the endless kit online,' Rhiane advises. 'My bare essentials are: a Berghaus Parvati waterproof jacket and Leylur trekking leggings.'

Do respect the great outdoors.

Rhiane notes that leaving the natural world as you found it is the only way to do a hike. 'It's little things like picking up your litter, closing gates on public footpaths, not walking on private land, but also not putting a banana peel on the floor and believing it's fine there because that's not the natural habitat for it to be in,' she explains.

Don't culturally appropriate.

The exchange of ideas, styles and traditions is one of the tenets and joys of a modern, multicultural society. But adopting the cultural signifiers of a marginalised group for your own amusement is never cool. If you're abroad and want to join in on local festivities, ask yourself a few questions. Is this item of religious, political or social significance to this community? Am I a part of a group or country that has historically benefitted from this community's subjugation? If the answers to these questions are 'yes', then step away from the sari, girl. Sasha recommends not wearing any cultural adornments if you're not from that country.

'Unless I have lived in a place and got to really know the culture or I have a direct relationship with that country or someone there, I don't wear anything because it's like painting up someone's traditional markings,' she notes.

Sasha explains that you can re-gift any indigenous items back to locals or simply take the items home instead of wearing them. So forgo the geisha costumes in Japan, forget the fake moustaches for Cinco de Mayo and don't imitate Native Americans by wearing headdresses. Remember that the locals should always be front and centre of their own celebrations, so if you are taking part, be respectful and think of yourself as merely an appreciative spectator.

Don't expect five-star treatment everywhere.

When heading to an economically deprived area, the rules are simple: don't be a dick. Don't complain unless your health, safety or finances have been truly compromised. Being a dick to the service people earning one-eighteenth of your monthly salary could impact entire communities and destroy businesses long after you leave.

You can re-gift any indigenous items back to locals or simply take the items home instead of wearing them.

Do interact with people beyond their role.

As Jessica Nabongo notes, your dialogues with service workers abroad don't have to be limited to their job.

'I like to interact with people in their given roles,' Jessica explains. 'So a bartender or a hotel worker can also tell me what's good in their country, what life is like for them.'

Treat people as more than just their job, and they'll treat you as more than just a tourist.

Do remember it's a tricky time to travel.

The coronavirus has everyone on edge – so be kind! On my flight to Lisbon in 2020, I was seated next to a girl with no mask and found myself assuming that she must be breaking the rules. It turned out she had a doctor's note and was exempt, but because I was so paranoid, I had quickly judged her. She later apologised for not informing me first, and I apologised for jumping to conclusions. Speak up if you feel someone is making you feel unsafe when travelling, but try not to let fear dictate your mood.

Do allow your worldview to widen.

When I was visiting a museum in Santo Domingo in my early twenties, I remember being struck by the portrayal of Christopher Columbus. In Britain's history books, Columbus is a revered explorer, but in the Dominican Republic, he's a ruthless colonial trespasser responsible for bringing disease and cruelty to the island and wiping out the native Taino people. So who's lyin' here? Well, the British, obviously. History is written by the 'winners', so when you travel elsewhere, don't expect your version to hold weight.

Similarly in South Africa, I remember being shocked at how a white tour guide held the British slave trader Cecil Rhodes in such high esteem when I'd learned only of his barbarity. Always be prepared to face a different version of history when you are in museums and tours abroad. Keep your mind open and remind yourself that your worldview is not universal.

Don't take basic travel photos.

Always obtain permission from the person whose photo you're taking before you snap. When in a building of historical or religious significance, always check that cameras are allowed. Seek permission from any minor's parents before including them in a picture. Don't be one of those people who poses with underprivileged children while volunteering and writes about their subsequent 'enlightenment'. You don't have to be white to have a saviour complex!

Don't be offended if someone asks you for money in exchange for a photo; this is totally normal in many parts of Vietnam, Bali, Cuba and other countries. You are taking something from them, and posing for tourists is a source of income they depend on. However, it's not always sustainable, so try bartering with pens and notebooks instead, or offer to email or print a copy of their picture.

Do romance responsibly.

PSA: sex tourism isn't just for old white dudes anymore! Plenty of black women flock to European countries to arrange romantic rendezvous. In Italy, there are even tours that cater to this growing demand. The power dynamics within such relationships require further unpacking elsewhere, but if you are dating a Cuban papi/mami or have a Bali bae, remember that cultural differences will impact your relationship. Expect certain things to get lost in translation (try not to misread *all the signs* like Bella from *I May Destroy You*). Expect a difference in sex/romance norms and expect to be relied upon financially at times. Lay out expectations and boundaries clearly from the start, and be clear on what you want. Oh, and always wrap it up, people.

Do watch your valuables.

Only bring essentials out during daytrips and at night. When staying in locations where petty theft is common, consider only taking your phone and camera out to reduce the risk. Got serious drip? Don't be flashy in poorer countries. Store your valuables in hotel/hostel safes and buy padlocks for lockers and suitcases.

Do research with your phone.

When you have Wi-Fi, find your chosen area on Google Maps and select 'download offline map' to navigate around without using up your data or attracting attention. You can also use Google Translate's audio function to communicate with locals in a different language. To keep Wi-Fi costs low during longer trips, find a plan with free global roaming before you leave, purchase a local SIM card when you land or consider renting or buying a portable Wi-Fi hotspot.

Do turn off your phone sometimes.

Don't be that person scrolling through the 'Gram on an idyllic boat trip in a sub-tropical paradise. And refrain from pulling out your phone in places where it's likely to draw attention. Not only will you miss out on some of the most eclectic sights, smells and sounds of your new surroundings if you're always on your phone, but it's also hella dangerous to make yourself a target by flashing expensive technology.

When you have Wi-Fi, download your chosen area on Google Maps so you can navigate without using up your data or attracting unwanted attention.

Do always carry cash with you on dates (and everywhere).

Familiarise yourself with carrying and using cash abroad because Venmo, Cash App and Apple Pay might not cut it in countries that aren't digital-first. Annette Richmond notes that she always keeps American dollars on her or in her room, and for dates, she believes cash is particularly important.

'Picture this: you're in a random country and back at someone's place after a date. But you're not feeling it anymore and don't want to be indebted to that person, so you decide to leave. But it's 3am, you have no money, and now you're out in the street. If you had cash, you'd be fine because it keeps you safe. Money will talk for you when there's a language barrier.'

She's too right!

Do dictate your boundaries when it comes to 'othering'.

I'll go a bit more in depth with this in the 'Travelling while black' chapter, but solo adventuring as a black woman in spaces where black people are few and far between can result in a set of particularly unique interactions. It's up to you to decide which of them are racialised and/or malicious in intent.

As Annette notes, 'I've got some friends who say they feel like a zoo animal if people ask for pictures with them abroad, so I'm not here to talk them into it. Personally I try and feel a vibe each time. You know the energy when someone wants to take a picture and make fun of you and has an attitude and when there's excitement and it's genuine.'

Do consider your carbon footprint.

Travel overland if you can. A Eurostar train from London to Paris emits around 90% less carbon than flying. Choose a tour provider like Intrepid or Geckos, who have offset their carbon emissions by purchasing carbon credits associated with renewable energy projects. When you arrive, choose public transport over private.

Jessica Nabongo explains, 'In hotel rooms, trash cans are lined with plastic, and if anything is in there, they replace the whole bag. Limit your use of the trash can to one so plastic bags are not used unnecessarily.'

You can also turn off the lights and air-con when you don't need them, bring backpacks when souvenir shopping, carry a reusable water bottle with you and eat sustainably and locally. During hikes, stay off protected land and always stick to the marked paths. If you're doing group tours, as Sasha Sarago advises, always 'choose companies whose eco-ethos are embedded in their principles. Check how much they pay local providers and the indigenous people they work with and whether they have eco-travel options.'

Do ask strangers to take your pictures.

If you're not in the habit of staging a professional shoot on your trip, then you're going to have to rely on the kindness of strangers, and honestly, it's luck of the draw. But for your best bet in securing bomb pics, 1) be polite, 2) show the person how you would ideally take a photo by framing for them first and 3) hope for the best!

Do engage with different types of travellers.

You've come halfway across the world only to find yourself primarily staying indoors, ordering room service and chilling by a pool listening to American music and speaking English. What was the point? Everyone deserves time to switch off, but solo travel is meant to broaden your horizons too. Get out there and meet people!

Always research what safety methods you can use in the country you're going to before you arrive so you don't end up in trouble.

— ANNETTE RICHMOND

Do check local protection laws.

Some solo travellers like to carry items, such as defensive
sprays and tasers, to protect themselves, but these aren't
legal everywhere. Annette Richmond used to carry pepper
spray with her at all times until a near-miss experience made
her more careful about packing it in her suitcase.

'A guy was following me around in Malaysia, he had pulled
his dick out, and he was making kissing noises at me. There
weren't a lot of people around, so I thought I was going to
have to use my pepper spray. In the end, I didn't, and it's just
as well because I later found out it's illegal in Malaysia. I could
have ended up in jail for trying to protect myself.'

Her advice? 'Always research what safety methods you can
use in the country you're going to before you arrive so you
don't end up in trouble.'

Do remember you are an unaccompanied woman.

Cultural norms differ around the world, and unfortunately, a
black woman travelling alone may still be viewed as highly
unusual or suspicious in some places. (FYI: I've been mistaken
for a prostitute in both Santo Domingo and Havana.) Do not
take offence at such assumptions; disarming people with a
warm smile or a simple correction in English is often enough.

But in cases where someone is making you feel uneasy,
just get the hell out of there. If you're being hassled, lying
and saying you're married works almost every time. Regularly
update friends and family back home of your whereabouts.
Favour taxi apps over random cabs. Research local customs,
the political climate and attitudes toward women in every
country before you arrive. Above all else, always trust
your instincts.

Q&A WITH
Annette Richmond

Facebook / Instagram: Fat Girls Traveling
Website: fromannette.com

California native and award-winning content creator Annette Richmond is also the founder of the body positive travel communities, Fat Girls Traveling and Fat Camp, as well as the Editor-in-Chief of Fat Girls Guide.

What have you learned from being a digital nomad for three years?
People are more kind than not. If I'm lost, there's always some kind soul who will help me work out where the fuck I am, and that can lead to an offer of dinner or they become a lifelong friend. And also, I love learning.

> *Black people are doing well in the media, so people are excited to see us in real life. That makes me excited too, but I don't always feel the pressure to be the smiling black face that 'yeses' them.*

What safety tips have you learned?

I share my location with local friends and friends back home on WhatsApp. I travel with a hard-shell suitcase with a padlock. l read every single review for accommodation, starting with the negative ones, and I stay in girls-only dorms. I also connect with strangers in the Girls Love Travel Facebook group!

How do you deal with unwanted attention in spaces where you stand out?

I experience most racial discrimination at home in America, and with size, it's abroad. If someone has a problem with my body, that's their problem because I'm fine as shit! In Asia, people will stand in line and take photos with me; they've never seen a fat, black person with blue braids before! I try to feel a person's energy; if I feel comfortable in that moment, then cool.

Black, female, plus-size travellers are still underrepresented online and abroad. Do you feel a responsibility to uphold a certain image?
I'll be abroad, and a person will yell out 'Nicki Minaj' or 'Oprah', and I think black excellence has a lot to do with that. Black people are doing well in the media, so people are excited to see us in real life. That makes me excited too, but I don't always feel the pressure to be the smiling black face that 'yeses' them. My role in this world is not to take pictures with every black person. We're not a monolith.

Why did you start Fat Girls Traveling?

Plus-size travellers don't see ourselves represented online, and if no one's willing to put themselves out there and be honest about the obstacles we face, then fat people won't travel. The honest truth is fat travel is more difficult. Kayaks have weight limits; with water sports, you need to think about scuba gear and life jackets that fit; on a plane, you may have to buy two or three seats. Once, I went to Bali, and the harness didn't fit around my waist for a swing. The next year, I found one that holds up to 400lbs, and I took girls from Fat Girls Traveling, and we all took pictures. I share my experiences but also create a platform that provides information so more fat people can go ziplining or kayaking or whatever. I also offer the platform to other people who are skydiving and doing shit that I'm not about to do!

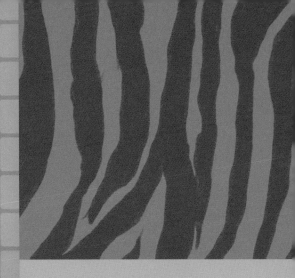

CHAPTER 4

How to be alone abroad – and love it

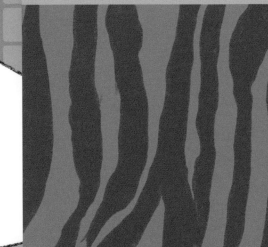

HOW TO BE ALONE ABROAD – AND LOVE IT

Once you transcend to a place of true self-trust, you will learn to love showing up alone and abroad.

A S A SOLO TRAVELLER, it's up to you to orchestrate your own adventure. You, and you alone, are responsible for seizing spontaneous moments and seeking out spaces that will nourish your very best self; nobody else can lead the way. But of course, that also means there's no one else to blame (I repeat: no one) if things don't go according to plan.

Solo travel necessitates being totally comfortable in your solitude, and while that doesn't happen overnight, there are ways to become the person who can show up to a three-day hike in the Colombian mountains, waltz unaccompanied into a packed bar in Berlin, or start a non-awkward conversation with the person next to you during a hostel breakfast. You first need to learn how to trust in yourself.

Self-trust means relying on your own integrity. It means understanding your decisions and letting go of regret when those decisions don't turn out perfectly. It means practising kindness toward yourself and others, singing along to 'Me, Myself and I' and really feeling every damn word. Self-trust is understanding your power as well as your limits.

Trusting yourself wholeheartedly while travelling alone also means setting yourself free from the approval of those who don't share your vision. It means recognising and removing yourself from any testing situations that might arise and creating moments that enrich your soul and bring you closer to the best version of yourself.

Once you trust yourself, solo travel will feel like less of a challenge and more like second nature. Instead of sitting lonesome in your hotel room lamenting your decision and avoiding all eye contact with everyone because you hate how self-conscious your solitude makes you feel, you'll actually learn to bask in it like a warm day in the sun. Trusting yourself on the road means understanding that even if things don't live up to your expectations, you still have yourself and you alone are the best company you could ask for. Once you transcend to a place of true self-trust, you will learn to love showing up alone where an unending world of possibility awaits.

But I get it; that shit can be scary sometimes! I'm a Londoner, so chatting to strangers is entirely unnatural and breaks many of us out in nervous hives, but trusting myself to make connections with others has enriched my travels tenfold. Sure, there are still times I get travel fatigue and blocking out the world with my headphones seems easier than exuding some Rihanna-level confidence, but knowing that I'm good if all else fails has awakened an in inner confidence in me that I never knew I had.

So, here are some tips to help even the most introverted and reluctant solo women enjoy eating, partying and talking to new people abroad.

Eating out alone

For me, pure indulgence comes in the form of enjoying a meal for one totally undisturbed. It's luxe. It's a total boss bitch move. And it means you can savour every last morsel. What is better than digging into teriyaki noodles for one, your mouth free from small talk, your tongue reserved only for flavour, as you watch the world fly by? Eating alone can mean curling up in a corner booth with a book or ordering a la carte for a private bedroom feast. Whatever you prefer, let go of the shame associated with eating alone with these tips:

▶ **DON'T OVERTHINK IT.**
Remember that each of us learned how to feed ourselves
from a young age. Eating alone is vital for self-nourishment,
and it definitely doesn't make you a weirdo. Remind yourself
of why you've taken yourself out (you're hungry, you want to
experience a new place, etc.) and what you're gaining from it
(food, fun, good memories). No one in public will be paying
you half as much attention as you think, hun.

▶ **BEFRIEND THE STAFF.**
Chat to your servers! Not only will you likely get better food
and service, but you can also obtain loads of local insider
knowledge too.

Reality is what

—Sampa the Great,

ou make it.

apper and songwriter

▶ **START SMALL.**
Build up your confidence. Depending on your expertise (and how audacious a solo traveller you are), there's definitely levels to eating out alone:

New to this solo eating thang? Beginners can try brunch, coffee or a grab-and-go meal. Cafes, food trucks and food courts offer casual seating, and it's easy to blend into the backdrop or strike up conversations with other diners.

When you're feeling a little braver, try a sit-down meal at a fancier place. I love a lunchtime set menu because it's cheaper and is usually more informal. I also check photos online first to catch a vibe.

If you fancy yourself a solo dining aficionado, don't forgo a fancy restaurant experience at night. Sit bang smack in the middle of all the action and soak up the ambience.

▶ **SIT AT THE BAR.**
This is the number one way to interact with those around you. Try striking up a conversation with the bartender about what to order and where you're from, and ask for food or travel recommendations.

▶ **BE MINDFUL.**
Mindfulness is the practice of concentrating on your thoughts and feelings in the present moment, and it lends itself perfectly to solo dining. I love to savour the sights, smells and tastes of the food I eat. Treat eating alone as a meditative experience.

▶ **LOOK BUSY.**
Feeling uber awkward in a restaurant? Entertain yourself. Bring a book, watch movies, listen to music on your phone or make a phone call to loved ones back home.

▶ **PEOPLE-WATCH.**
Watching the intricacies of people and places unfold as you eat can prove to be endlessly fascinating. But remember that observing works both ways; if you want to be inconspicuous, sit in the corner or back of a restaurant.

▶ **ENJOY IT.**
Order room service in bed and relish every bite. Treat each solo meal as an unapologetic celebration of yourself.

I love a lunchtime set menu because it's cheaper and is usually more informal. I also check photos online first to catch a vibe.

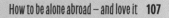

Nightlife

Tackling a party destination without a friend by your side can be daunting, but with a little practice, you'll be strutting into bars, clubs and boats like a bad B.

▶ **STAY IN A HOSTEL.**
Hostels, although not for everyone, are the absolute best way to meet other travellers. I've lost count of the number of nights I've spent with strangers, talking about our lives while lying in hammocks, swapping music recommendations or playing drinking games. After you've embraced the small talk in-house, attending outside events and bars will come more naturally. Plus, you'll have a ready-made group to go out with.

▶ GET SOCIAL IN THE DAYTIME.

Bike trips, walking tours, wine tasting, cooking classes and hikes are just some of the daytime activities you can take advantage of to meet others. Swap details with your new friends in the day and make plans for the evening.

▶ PICK SOMETHING YOU LOVE.

To increase the likelihood of having a damn good time, only do things that truly interest you. It's good to leave your comfort zone, but if you really hate museums, don't go alone and rely on meeting someone there to have a good time. Take the pressure off yourself; it's your trip after all.

▶ DON'T RELY ON STRANGERS.

It's easy to get swept up in the romance of a new night-time best friend, but when travelling alone, always put yourself first. You can't always rely on someone you've just met to help you out if things go wrong. Got a bad feeling about the venue? Leave. Don't want to be dragged into that round of shots? Don't drink it. Always have your route home planned before you go out, be extra vigilant of your valuables and never get too drunk if you're someplace unfamiliar.

▶ BOUNCE BACK.

Sometimes an evening just doesn't go as planned; conversations feel forced, the music doesn't bang and you feel overly self-conscious. It happens. But don't let one flop put you off braving a bar alone in the future. No two nights are ever the same.

Try to live your life
will not regret years
inertia and timidity
choices ... pick up the
it a better world,

—Maya Angelou

n a way that you of useless virtue and ... You make your own battle and make ust where you are.

poet, writer and activist

Online meet-ups

Swipe and message your way to a new best friend. Online meet-ups are great for vetting people and getting to the heart of a local community.

▶ **APPS**
Try the Couchsurfing app to make friends and land free accommodations, and use the Meetup app to find events in your new area.

▶ **DATING**
Meet a foreign cutie. Tinder is a global app after all...

▶ **FACEBOOK GROUPS**
Annette Richmond favours Facebook groups filled with locals to meet other like-minded travellers.

'I felt safe finding friends in a group like 'Girls Love Travel' or my group 'Fat Girls Traveling', which has 13,000 members because it's all women. You can say, "Hey, I'm going to be in Bali" and then you have a friend who is a local and a traveller. I've done that a lot of times. When that person is abroad, they want the same experience, so you find lots of people who are really willing to help out.'

Annette has facilitated many meet-ups in different countries.

'My members have met each other everywhere,' she says. 'It's a little less daunting than sitting in a bar and talking to a random.'

Rhiane Fatinikun of Black Girls Hike also recommends joining a travel community. 'The thought of venturing out alone can be quite daunting, so where do you find hiking friends? Social media is great! Make sure you follow groups such as Black Girls Hike as we host meet ups across the UK for women of all ages. I've met so many people and we are just growing and growing!'

I felt safe finding friends in a group like 'Girls Love Travel' or my group 'Fat Girls Traveling', which has 13,000 members, because it's all women.

— **ANNETTE RICHMOND**

7 fearless ways to start conversations abroad

It's time to embrace the small talk with these perfect conversation starters compiled to not only help you break the ice but improve your chances of making real connections with the people around you. Don't worry! Most people won't think you're a weirdo. And the ones who do ain't worth talking to anyway.

Remember: always be polite and wait for a suitable moment before interjecting. Be sure to smile, maintain good eye contact and avoid bragging about what you do back home or how much travelling you've already done (it's boring). Happy friend-hunting!

1

AT A BAR, CAFE OR RESTAURANT BEFORE ORDERING
"Excuse me. What's that you're eating/drinking? Would you recommend it?"

2

OFFER A COMPLIMENT AND FOLLOW UP
"That's a nice backpack/dog/head of fresh box braids! Where did you get them? Are you travelling solo? Do you live around here?"

> *Don't worry! Most people won't think you're a weirdo. And the ones who do ain't worth talking to anyway.*

OBSERVE AND FOLLOW UP
"Excuse me. I noticed you're reading the same book as me right now. Do you like it?

Hey, I've got a very similar camera to yours. Are you a professional photographer?

I really like your [insert object here]. Did you buy it here?"

LISTEN IN AND FOLLOW UP
"Excuse me, but I overheard you talking about [insert activity here]. I've just been there/seen that. Do you want some tips?

Hey, I heard you're from [insert city/country here]. So am I!"

ASKING A LOCAL FOR HELP
"Hello! My language skills aren't too great. Do you know what this word means? Could you help me translate this, please?"

6
ASKING A LOCAL FOR TIPS

"Hi! Could you tell me what's fun to do around here? I'm visiting for the weekend.

Excuse me, is [insert attraction/town here] worth visiting? My guidebook says yes, but I'd love a local's opinion."

7
WHEN YOU'RE FEELING BRAVE/APPROACHING A GROUP:

"Excuse me, I'm travelling by myself. Would you mind if I joined you? Hey, where are you guys from? I'm from [insert city/country here], but I'm here alone for the week; could I sit with you? Mind if I pull up a seat?"

Q&A WITH
Rhiane Fatinikun

Instagram: @bgh_uk
Facebook: Black Girls Hike - UK

Rhiane, a 33-year-old Manchester-based Brit, founded Black Girls Hike in 2019 after a solo jaunt to the Peak District (a national park in central England) inspired her to get other black women enjoying the great outdoors. Black Girls Hike has quickly spiralled into a movement, bringing solo walkers together for group trips around the UK.

Why did you start Black Girls Hike?

In January 2019, I made a video on a train ride home through the Peak District saying, 'I'm taking up hiking #BGH', then later, I set up the Instagram page, and it took off. I wanted to create a space for women to express their love of nature in a like-minded community. Also, being black in the UK is mainly centred on the London experience. I'm based in

Manchester, and we do our walks in the Peak District, but it's nice to attract people from all over. We now have leaders in the Midlands and London, and we eventually want to do international trips.

What benefits are there to hiking on your own?
When you're alone, you can be more present with your thoughts. Sometimes I listen to music (I listen to reggae or soca, so it's always a vibe!), but other times, I don't use headphones so I can really appreciate the sounds of nature.

What has hiking taught you about the world around you?
It has taught me how beautiful the countryside is, and I want to appreciate it and protect it more. I'm also reminded that we need to talk about how black and brown people are disproportionately affected by climate change. Hiking allows me to connect more with the world around me.

How have people responded to Black Girls Hike?
At first, the response was 'hiking?' but people are really enthusiastic, and since the pandemic started, people have come for the well-being factor too. For many, it's been something they've never really thought about doing before. We complain that the UK is really cold, but it's a beautiful country, and there's lots to see. People come to build their confidence and fitness, and we attract a good mix of people: women in their sixties, teenagers, women with dogs, etc.

The outdoors is different for everybody, but hiking is a thing black women haven't really been socialised to do.

Are there barriers that have prevented black women from exploring the great outdoors?

You don't really see black people hiking in the media, and most black people live in inner cities. In the UK, lots of historical buildings have slavery backgrounds too, and because of that, hiking has a very middle-class background. The outdoors is different for everybody, but hiking is a thing black women haven't really been socialised to do. In school, it was always basketball, American football, athletics, or running. I want to make hiking more inclusive.

Where is the best place to hike in the UK?

I love the Welsh coast! The entire coast is well sign-posted and stretches over 800 miles. I started in central Swansea, went to Oxwich Bay, Rhossili Bay, then finished in Port Eynon. The locals were so friendly, and the scenery was amazing. If you want to explore the Peak District, the village of Edale is also a great base that's surrounded by lush, green hills.

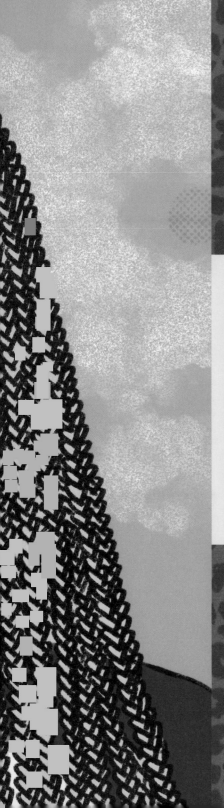

CHAPTER 5

Travelling while black

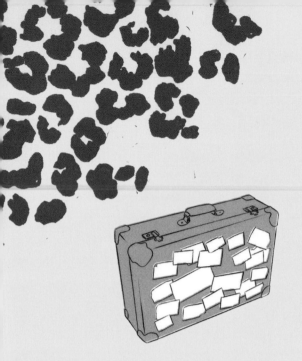

TRAVELLING
WHILE BLACK

*Black women deserve to go where we
are not only tolerated but accepted
and celebrated.*

RESTRICTION OF movement is something many western travellers have not had to consider before COVID-19. For many individuals, being able to go wherever, whenever is an intrinsic part of passport privilege that many take for granted. We have normalised the idea of banning citizens from less economically developed countries, but never stopped to consider the possibility of that reality becoming inverted. But life comes at you fast, right? And suddenly, powerful states are dealing with the reality of being unable to cross the borders of the places they once restricted access from.

But many black travellers already understand the anxiety that comes with not belonging in certain spaces or experiencing hyper-surveillance simply because of an unchangeable aspect of our identities. Often it is a part of travelling while black.

Black experiences abroad vary greatly depending on a myriad of factors, including accent, gender, nationality, stature, skin tone and passport privilege. For solo black female travellers, standing out abroad can also threaten our safety and sense of self. Our presence abroad can elicit shock, awe and fascination in places where a black woman travelling unaccompanied is seen as a novelty act that defies trends. In some cases, it can also result in discrimination or 'othering'.

But – say it with me now – black women deserve to go where we are not only tolerated but accepted and celebrated.

When planning a trip, choosing a place where the political climate toward foreign travellers is generally welcoming is important, but remember, this does not guarantee a totally

If you travel to a majority-black country, you will have the fascinating opportunity to learn more about your place within a unified global community.

smooth ride. You may also want to consider local relations to the diasporic community, as well as anecdotal accounts of individual treatment from other black travellers. All of this will help you curate your own travel experience that is unforgettable for all the right reasons. But don't forget that individual acts of discrimination are perpetuated by individuals and are in no way representative of a whole country. And oftentimes, race relations in so-called 'first-world' countries can be far worse than they are in our chosen travel destinations.

Travelling while black is an incredibly enriching experience, providing you with the chance to educate and be educated and expand your cultural horizons. And if you travel to a majority-black country, you will have the fascinating opportunity to learn more about your place within a unified global community and draw from vibrant and adaptive cultures.

Here are a few potential scenarios you may need to consider, as well as advice on how to handle them if they occur.

You may need to research the racial climate of your chosen destination.

Search for stories from black bloggers and locals before you arrive to gain insight into the experiences of others like you. Try to seek out both positive and negative experiences, as well as the general vibe of the diasporic community. It's also worth considering the residency status of the author of such materials and how long you will be staying, because visiting for a week is totally different from living somewhere and attempting to integrate. Would one or two accounts of racism toward someone on a week-long visit put you off from visiting entirely? It shouldn't.

Travelling while black is an incredibly enriching experience, providing you with the chance to expand your cultural horizons.

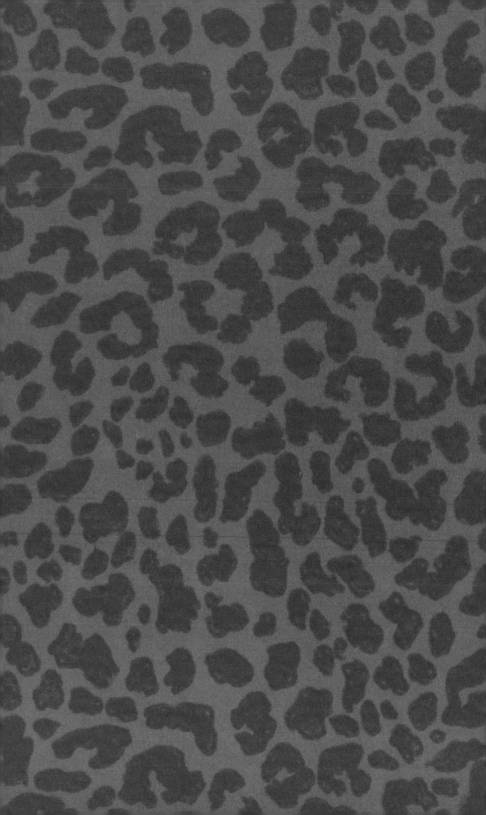

Don't let fear stop you from fulfilling your travel story.

In times of increased violence against black bodies, it is natural to feel hesitant about venturing to a new country where there are fewer black people than you are used to, but the world is wide and exciting! And after travelling extensively, I believe most people within it are good. A snapshot blog post won't ever give you a full picture of life in that place, and ultimately, opinions can only be formed once you arrive. Don't let fear stop you from fulfilling your travel story.

As Rhiane Fatinikun notes, if she'd let fear dictate, she would never have started hiking. 'There's loads of stereotypes around black people and nature which you just need to ignore,' she says. 'Even when I told people I wanted to hike they were like, what? But I wanted to create a space for black women and I'm so glad that I did.'

You may get asked for pictures.

Let's fast-forward to the islands. Your skin is gold (no spray tan), your outfit is co-ordinated and the box braids are fresh. That in and of itself is enough of a reason for others to want to snap a photo of you. But it may also be related to your status as the only visible minority around, so how do you react?

Well, it is totally up to you. If a sneaky photo makes you uncomfortable, then ask the person to stop or use clear hand signals if they can't understand you (no is the same in every language!). If you're enjoying the limelight, why not use the moment to jump-start a cultural conversation or ask them to take your new 'Gram photo afterward? I'm personally of the opinion that being a racial spectacle can never lead to racial acceptance, so posing with strangers simply because I'm black and they're curious doesn't sit well with me. But everyone's different. You do you, boo.

You may find other aspects of your identity add to your experiences.

Black women aren't a monolith, and each of us will find vastly different experiences abroad based on where we are in the world and the many complex ways our blackness intersects with other facets of our identity. If you belong to other minority groups, such as plus size, LGBTQIA+, indigenous or disabled, you may find more hyper-surveillance in places where you are a visible racial other.

Annette Richmond of Fat Girls Traveling believes it is her size, not her race, that results in more attention abroad.

'A lot of aggression because of my race happens in America where I'm from, but when it comes to my size, that is a bigger deal abroad. They are much more focused on this in Asia. Kids will point and stare, and people will laugh.'

Research the attitudes of your chosen country toward your particular identity groups to help you feel more confident about travelling.

In times of increased violence against black bodies, it is natural to feel hesitant about venturing to a new country - but the world is wide and exciting!

You may attract racialised attention.

Every woman deals with unwanted sexualised attention whether at home or abroad, but for black women, this can take on a racialised tone, which can feel unsettling. If you are being made to feel like a racial spectacle abroad and you don't like it, head somewhere safe, crowded and touristy, like a cafe or restaurant, and centre yourself. Journal, call a friend, plan the next part of your trip and remember that one bad experience does not characterise a whole country!

When I was in Fez, Morocco, with a week-long, all-white tour group, cries of 'Beyoncé' and 'Serena Williams' followed me around the meandering streets. Now while I was both flattered and bewildered at being compared to two of the world's hottest, most successful babes, I don't exactly bear a strong resemblance to either. I realised that while I was in North Africa, women who looked like me were still a rarity, and the hyper-visibility of African Americans and their culture was so prevalent that most locals simply assumed I was from the States.

The unwanted attention became irritating after a while, but I stayed close to my tour guide and rested up in my hotel when I felt overwhelmed. And once I accepted that my presence in Morocco was eliciting a reaction that was not entirely negative but, rather, based on a narrow perception of blackness and black people, I continued enjoying my trip without taking the comments personally.

You may get mistaken for a local.

When travelling in a majority-black country, you may pass as a local, which will give you a fascinating insight into the intricacies and inner workings of diasporic communities around the world. Embrace it! Passing as a local can result in invisibility, which brings about benefits. You may move through spaces undetected, pay less for market items or travel on public transport with ease.

When I was in Cuba, passing as a local also meant building quicker bonds with local people, avoiding being hassled in the most touristy parts of Havana and using the local currency. But passing as a local can also remove the visible layer of protection that comes with being a tourist. You may find you are privy to how locals are treated and receive a lower level of service in bars and restaurants or be refused entry to entertainment venues in favour of others.

Relish each role you are able to play as a black traveller in a black country, enjoy the process of passing as a tourist, a local and back again and be grateful for the insight you can obtain in both worlds. Your travels and level of cultural understanding will be so much deeper because of it.

Relish each role you are able to play as a black traveller in a diasporic community. Enjoy the process of passing as a local. Be grateful for the insight you obtain in both worlds.

Passport privilege can be experienced by anyone, but when you are black, it can be disconcerting to receive perks that appear to transcend your race.

You may experience passport privilege.

Being black and owning a passport from a western country often results in better treatment abroad than it does for black nationals from poorer nations who suffer from more negative stigma. Jessica Nabongo has travelled on both her Ugandan and American passports and discovered vast differences in how she was treated.

'I've entered countries like Fiji on both passports, and I saw the discrimination. I entered on an American passport and was treated better.'

Jessica believes that her 'travelling as a well-to-do person on an African passport might spark something in someone's mind in those immigration booths'.

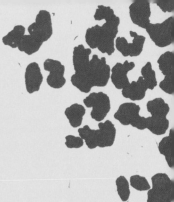

Keep your privilege in perspective.

Anti-black sentiment is more pertinent for black travellers from Africa than it is for black Brits or African Americans, and that is because of the perceived power of our national identities abroad, a privilege associated with our passports. You may notice black locals working in low-paid service roles or enduring racial persecution in some countries abroad, while you, on the other hand, experience preferential treatment in airports, bars, restaurants and other public spaces because of your nationality and accent.

Passport privilege can be experienced by anyone (and is often synonymous with whiteness), but when you are black, it can be disconcerting to receive perks that appear to transcend your race. Many of our home countries (the so-called 'first-world nations') are so racially polarised that it may take leaving and being abroad to really feel this privilege. This is something Annette Richmond innately understands.

'In Mexico, I'm an American. But in America, I'm just a black person,' she says. 'If something happened to me in Latin America, there would be noise, and the embassy would get involved, but at home, I'd just be part of a system. I only have American passport privileges when I leave America.'

Be aware of this as you travel and always keep your privilege in perspective.

Q&A WITH
Sasha Sarago

Instagram: @ascensionmag
Website: ascensionmag.com

Sasha Sarago is the founder of **Ascension** *magazine in Australia and has lived in the States. She is a strong advocate for Aboriginal Australian women.*

Where do you gather inspiration for your trips? And how do you travel?

I love Travel Noire and Instagram! As a traveller, I'm very independent, but I like things to be structured, so I like doing group tours, and when I've done a few days and gathered some tips from the travel guide, then I go off and do my own thing.

What's the most important thing you have learned from your travels?

Always trust your instincts. For the majority of the time, you might be in a physical space that's different from home, so trust your gut because it's your personal compass. Be aware of your surroundings and your energy. Also bring out that alter ego and act a little more confident. I carry myself a little more confidently when I'm abroad.

How does your identity change as you travel?

I get more respect for my Aboriginal culture when I'm outside of Australia. People are more interested, so I can really show who I am. But when I'm at home, there's the baggage of colonisation and how white people consider my culture a think piece, and I'm yelling, 'Hear me, see me'. Travel allows me to be myself.

How do you interact authentically with local people?

I think research is key. Whether you're looking at what the price range is to haggle with locals, checking where the products in your accommodation are from or asking locals where to go beyond the touristy setup, it's always great to get a local perspective.

I get more respect for my Aboriginal culture when I'm outside of Australia. People are more interested, so I can really show who I am ... Travel allows me to be myself.

CHAPTER 6

28 tips for travel budgeting

28 TIPS FOR TRAVEL BUDGETING

Financial planning never looked so easy.

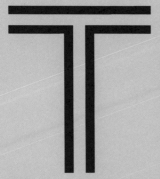

TO PARAPHRASE A very wise woman, if you wanna do rich shit you need your money thick, thick. *Sticks out tongue in Megan Thee Stallion*

Now, I'm not saying travel is reserved for the uber-wealthy or that saving all year just to flex on Instagram for a 72-hour boat trip is a wise move. But solo travel certainly requires a level of financial security and pre-planning to feel truly free. No matter the length of your trip or your preferred travel style, a healthy bank balance will definitely take the pressure off.

I managed to save thousands back home before I hit the road. Granted, I had the privilege of living at home with family, but I also employed a few of the tactics below to make my money stretch a hell of a lot further once I was travelling.

Working at hostels, writing website copy and helping out in exchange for free room and board, as well as booking homestays and volunteer schemes where my food and room were all included, helped me plan ahead and save serious moolah for the full year I was away.

Financial advice is deeply personal and unique to each person. What works for one may not work for another, and of course, your desired travel style and personal circumstances will dictate how much you save and spend along the way.

So, I've put together 28 budgeting hacks for each stage of your travels, whether you're looking to save up, spend less or earn as you go.

No matter the length of your trip or your preferred travel style, a healthy bank balance will take the pressure off.

Saving up

Assess your expenditures and start cutting back on your spending months before you leave your home country.

1 CUT LIVING COSTS.

Moving back home with family is a great way to make huge savings on rent, but if living with family is not an option, you can find other ways to cut living costs, like renting out your spare room on Airbnb or getting a roommate. You could even sublet your room and sleep in the living room. When I travelled to NYC, I was a guest in someone's bedroom while my host slept on the couch for three months. It was fine for me and a great way for the host to save up quickly.

2 START HOSTING ON COUCHSURFING.

OK, so Couchsurfing largely benefits the guests more, but hear me out. If you start hosting people while you're living at home, by the time you hit the road, you may be able to call on your global network to return the favour or at least show you around. I did this before I left the UK and had ready-made friends when I needed them, which saved on socialising and accommodation costs. Think ahead, people!

3 CUT EXPENSES.

Serious about travel? Check your bank statement, write down a list of your monthly expenses and start cancelling those direct debits. Streaming sites, Amazon Prime, gym memberships, beauty subscription boxes, manicures – you could live without all these things for a few months.

4 REDUCE LUNCH COSTS.

Whether you're a lunch-on-the-go kinda gal or a coffee addict, you could be spending hundreds each month that could go toward your travel fund! I know the Chipotle/ Leon/KFC addiction is real, so first try cutting down your daily lunch spending first before deciding to bring your food entirely. FYI: if you eat out five times a week, just trimming your lunch costs from $12 to $8 saves you $832 a year!

We need to encourage
know that they are
destiny, that they have
to tell, and that they
of writing

—Michaela Coel, actress

black women to authors of their own important stories are capable ... them ...

screenwriter and director

5 TIME YOUR SUPERMARKET SHOPPING.

There's no shame in asking your local supermarket when they put out the discounted food then timing your weekly shop to nab some bargains. Food is one of the biggest expenses that can impede your travel budgeting plans, but it's also super easy to save on too. Be sure to freeze spare portions and delete the take-out apps from your phone.

6 ORGANISE CLOTHING SWAPS.

Fast fashion is not only bad for the planet but your wallet too. Before I began travelling, I deleted the shopping apps from my phone and started doing clothing swaps with friends. The premise is simple; each of you brings a bundle of outfits you're bored of, dump them into the middle of the room and get to swapping. You could also go to thrift stores, charity shops or turn to eBay or Depop for more bargains.

7 TRANSFER MONEY INTO YOUR SAVINGS EACH TIME YOU SAVE ON A PURCHASE.

This one requires a real mindset adjustment, but it's worth it. Each time you make a saving (i.e., pack your lunch instead of purchase one), transfer the money you would have spent into your savings account. I promise it will stack up quickly.

8 DIRECT DEBIT (DIRECT DEPOSIT) INTO YOUR SAVINGS.

Shop around for the best savings account. Look for one that offers freebies that suit you, like discounted gym memberships or train tickets. Make a monthly direct debit (direct deposit) the day you get paid to save money without thinking about it.

9 SIGN UP ON CASHBACK SITES.

I love getting paid for buying the things I need! Cashback sites work on referral links, meaning if you use their site to buy a laptop from your favourite retailer, they get a slice of the earnings and you get money off your purchase. I've received cashback on flights, electrical equipment, beauty products and more. The most I received was £40 off a £400 camera, so if you use cashback sites for large items, the discounts will come rolling in! Try TopCashback (US and UK), Quidco (UK), ShopBack (AU) or MyPoints (US), and install the Honey app on your browser.

10 SELL YOUR SKILLS ONLINE.

If you're looking to make money from home, why not start a side hustle? I know friends who have successful Etsy and eBay businesses (it takes a lot of work, of course). There's also sites, like Fiverr and Upwork, where you can sell your digital skills as a freelancer or find jobs in things like coding or writing.

Host people from Couchsurfing while you're living at home, and by the time you hit the road, you can call on your global network to return the favour.

On the road

Travel for free and cut back on spending abroad with these handy tricks.

11 GO WHERE YOUR CURRENCY IS STRONG.
A 'strong' dollar or pound in a certain country means your currency can buy more goods there. Annette Richmond of Fat Girls Travelling, who has been on the road for three years, says this is her number one tip.

'I'm a digital nomad who gets paid in American dollars, so I only go where the dollar is worth the most,' she says.

12 DON'T FORGET YOUR STUDENT ID.
I once forgot my ID in Rome, only to realise I could have saved majorly on admission prices to tourist attractions had I been better prepared. Many countries offer huge student discounts, especially in Europe, where you can get a Eurail Youth Pass for 25% less than a standard adult train ticket across the continent, or you can book through STA travel for discount travel packages.

13 VOLUNTEER.
I've volunteered for hostels in exchange for room and board, but you can also use sites like Volunteer Forever and Working Traveller to find specific schemes and programs.

14 **USE WORKAWAY.**
Workaway offers work exchanges, usually on hostels and farms around the world, for food and accommodation. I've used the site in Colombia, Nicaragua and Costa Rica and found it offers one-of-a-kind travel experiences while also saving me serious amounts of cash.

15 **BOOK LONG-TERM ACCOMMODATION FOR LONG-TERM TRIPS.**
As Annette notes, 'If you have a three-month visa for a country, book your accommodation for three months versus on a weekly basis because the longer you stay, the better deal you're going to get.'

16 **NEGOTIATE.**
You'd be surprised at how few people ask for upgrades, complimentary hotel breakfasts, extra airline baggage and other perks. But if you don't ask ... you don't get it! Tell people if you're a cash-strapped student or budget traveller and see what you can negotiate.

17 **CONSIDER HOUSE/PET-SITTING.**
Watch people's homes or pets for free, and you can nab free accommodation. Use a site like TrustedHousesitters, where everyone has to be verified.

18 **DO THE COUCHSURFING THING.**
Save on accommodation costs by sleeping for free in someone else's home. Always check your host's reviews and let others know your location before agreeing to a stay.

19 **OPT FOR LARGE HOSTEL ROOMS.**
Choosing hostels helps cut back on accommodation costs. A 12-person dorm will usually be cheaper than a four-person dorm, so pack those earplugs and make those savings.

20 **SEARCH FOR FREE STUFF.**
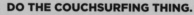
You'd be surprised how many free activities and events occur in major cities. Free walking tours and meet-ups are easy to find, but with a little planning, you can also locate free film showings, food and drink samples, exhibitions, shows and cultural events.

Ask for upgrades, complimentary hotel breakfasts, extra airline baggage and other perks. If you don't ask ... you don't get!

21 BROWSE INCOGNITO
Search engines and booking sites store your previous search history, so to ensure you are getting the best deal possible, turn your internet browser to incognito mode.

22 SET UP FLIGHT ALERTS.
Google Flights allows you to request email notifications if the price for your desired flight drops. I've used this tactic to snag flights several times. You can also sign up for Jack's Flight Club to receive weekly emails on the best global deals.

23 USE REFERRAL CREDITS.
New to Airbnb, Uber or Booking.com? Sign-up bonuses can help you save, but if you can't find any, look for referral codes from your favourite bloggers too.

24 BRING YOUR OWN WATER BOTTLE.
Water on the go can cost quite a bit abroad. Be sure to keep a refillable bottle with you at all times to save money as well as the environment.

25 STAND AT THE BAR.
Food and drinks in a continental European cafe is always much cheaper at the bar than at a table. An espresso in Florence might cost €1 at the bar but €2.50 if you sit at a table.

26 OPT FOR A FANCY LUNCH OVER A FANCY DINNER.
As I mentioned before, when dining solo, picking a fancy restaurant for lunch where there is often a set menu can save you loads without compromising on experience.

27 BOOK AHEAD.
Eating out on your own can be pricey, but websites like Trip Advisor and The Fork allow you to make huge savings on nice restaurants abroad just by booking ahead.

28 EARN FLYER MILES.
If you're a regular flyer, becoming a member of a frequent flyer program is a must. You can also collect flyer miles through credit cards, many of which offer huge sign-up bonuses. But always read the terms and conditions on these cards to avoid running up debt.

Now that you're stacking that cash with my advice, there's absolutely no excuse not to go ahead and plan your next adventure.

As I grew into
I began to indulge
to travel which
leave me while I have

—Mary Seacole, globa

womanhood
that longing
will never
health and vigour.

urse and traveller

CONCLUSION: NOW, IT'S TIME TO HIT THE ROAD

BLACK TRAVEL AND the conversations around it have marked an exciting shift in representation and self-actualisation all over the globe. For black women, travel is a tool of empowerment and self development, inching us ever closer to the kind of freedom we deserve. Through travel, we are able to explore the richness of our heritage and uncover the hidden parts of ourselves, becoming the voices of our travel narratives and helping those less fortunate than us carve out their dreams as well.

Remember this as you start planning your trip amidst an uncertain travel future – and follow me on Instagram (georginalawton_) and Twitter (@GeorginaLawton) and find my memoir, *Raceless*, on Amazon and in all popular bookstores, to keep up with my travel story as it continues to unfold.

I hope the information in this book has left you feeling more excited about the idea of solo travel, whether or not you end up venturing far. Solo travel isn't a destination; it's a state of being. It's building up your confidence and appreciating the smallest of trips, soaking up your company and taking notice of the people around you.

Adopt a travel state of mind and you'll find that every day presents itself as a universe of unending possibilities.

Good luck and safe travels!

Travel is a tool of empowerment and enrichment, inching us ever closer to the kind of freedom we deserve.

RESOURCES

Nomadness Travel Tribe

Nomadnesstv.com
IG: @nomadnesstribe
Founded by Evita Robinson in 2011, this travel community has grown to over 20,000 and today provides the blueprint for much of the black travel movement with trips and resources.

Jet Black

Globaljetblack.com
IG: @globaljetblack
Created by Jessica Nabongo (@thecatchmeifyoucan), this boutique luxury travel firm will help you design the trip of our dreams.

Gal-dem

Gal-dem.com

IG: @galdemzine

While not strictly a travel site, gal-dem, the award-winning magazine for women and non-binary people of colour, offers travel content that breaks the mould.

Fat Girls Traveling

Fatgirlstraveling.
wordpress.com

IG: @fatgirlstraveling

Fat activism through the travel lens comes in the form of this fabulous resource from Annette Richmond.

Black Girls Hike

Bghuk.com

IG: @bgh_uk

This hiking group of black women was founded by Rhiane Fatinikun to help women connect with nature and tackle the lack of representation in the great outdoors. The group now runs hikes and events all over the UK with plans to go global.

Dip Your Toes In

IG: @Dipyourtoesin

Couple creators Eulanda and Omo provide travel tips on their Instagram page alongside photography courses, food recommendations and brand pitching workshops.

ABC Travel Green Book

abctravelnetwork.com

This clever directory spotlights black-owned businesses all over the world. Founded by diversity consultant Martinique Lewis, the book contains restaurants, transport companies, tours and recreational spots and is a great way to connect all across the diaspora.

Black Girls Travel Too

Blackgirlstraveltoo.com
IG: @blackgirlstraveltoo
This online community
creates tools and tips to
inspire women to travel,
spotlighting marginalised
voices on its Instagram
page and organising trips
to Barbados, India and
South Africa.

Spirited Pursuit

IG: @spiritedpursuit
Lee Litumbe's envy-inducing
Instagram aesthetic alone
will make you quit your job
and move to Kenya, but the
influencer also offers social
media guides, retreats and
travel advice for much of the
African Continent.

Tastemakers Africa

Tastemakersafrica.com
IG: @tstmkrsafrica
With a safe escape resource
pack for pandemic-
friendly destinations, to
virtual experiences and
curated trips to Africa,
Tastemakers is an adaptive,
dynamic community for the
curious traveller.

Travel Noire

Travelnoire.com
IG: travelnoire
A boutique travel company
helping millennials discover,
plan and experience
international travel via group
trips, language lessons and
destination advice.

How Not To Travel Like A Basic Bitch

Hownottotravellikea basicbitch.com /
IG: @hownottotravellike abasicbitch

Dr. Kiona is all about education though travel, and she makes no apologies for uplifting the voices of marginalised folk on her page and also running ethical trips to Cuba with local input.

Travelingfro

Thetravelingfro.com
IG: @travelingfro

Jakiya Brown launched her brand the Travelingfro after quitting her '9-9' in New York City back in 2016. She's now based in Senegal where she runs authentic trips to East Africa and.teaches people how to grow, build and brand their own business, while living a life on their own terms.

Intrepid

Intrepidtravel.com
IG: @intrepidtravel

A leader in ethical travel since 1989, Intrepid puts together some of the most highly rated group trips and retreats around, with local leaders, exciting itineraries and offset carbon footprints.

ACKNOWLEDGEMENTS

A huge thank you to the interviewees featured in this book: Rhiane, Annette, Jessica, Sasha for their insight and advice.

I'd also like to thank my agent Zoe Ross at United for always championing my voice, and my brilliant editor Lyric Dodson for all her hard work and thoughtful suggestions.

A big thank you goes to my publishers, Hardie Grant, and in particular Megan and Melissa, for asking me to write this book, and in doing so, recognising that we need a more diverse range of voices in the travel sphere and wider publishing world.

A word of gratitude, also, to my friends and family, for putting up with my itchy feet and constant soul-searching for the last five years. And to anyone that has bought this book – thank you! I hope this book will help you walk wild and wonderful paths, inspiring you to travel beyond what you thought were your limits.

Published in 2021 by Hardie Grant Travel, a division of
Hardie Grant Publishing

Hardie Grant Travel (Melbourne)
Building 1, 658 Church Street
Richmond, Victoria 3121

Hardie Grant Travel (Sydney)
Level 7, 45 Jones Street
Ultimo, NSW 2007

www.hardiegrant.com/au/travel

NATIONAL LIBRARY OF AUSTRALIA — A catalogue record for this
book is available from the
National Library of Australia

Hardie Grant acknowledges the Traditional Owners of the country
on which we work, the Wurundjeri people of the Kulin nation and
the Gadigal people of the Eora nation, and recognises their continuing
connection to the land, waters and culture. We pay our respects to
their Elders past, present and emerging.

Black Girls Take World
ISBN 9781741177022

10 9 8 7 6 5 4 3 2 1

Publisher	Proofreader	Illustrator
Melissa Kayser	Anja Drayton	Rachelle Baker
Project editor	**Edtiorial assistance**	**Typesetting**
Megan Cuthbert	Rosanna Dutson	Megan Ellis
Editor	**Design**	
Lyric Dodson	Dian Holton	

Colour reproduction by Megan Ellis and Splitting Image Colour Studio
Printed and bound in China by LEO Paper Products LTD.

FSC
www.fsc.org
MIX
Paper from
responsible sources
FSC® C020056

The paper this book is printed on is certified
against the Forest Stewardship Council®
Standards and other sources. FSC® promotes
environmentally responsible, socially
beneficial and economically viable
management of the world's forests.